THE NATURE OF
REVELATION

BY

NATHAN SÖDERBLOM

Authorized Translation from the Second Edition of 1930

BY

FREDERIC E. PAMP

*

WITH AN INTRODUCTION BY

EDWARD CALDWELL MOORE, D.D., Th.D.

*Plummer Professor of Christian Morals Emeritus of
Harvard University and Chairman Emeritus
of the Board of Preachers to the University*

OXFORD UNIVERSITY PRESS
LONDON: HUMPHREY MILFORD

1933

Copyright, 1933, By
OXFORD UNIVERSITY PRESS
NEW YORK, INC.

Printed in the United States of America

TO

ANNA SÖDERBLOM

NÉE FORSELL

Introduction

THE death, a year ago, of Nathan Söderblom, Archbishop of Upsala, Primate of Sweden, was the loss to the world of learning of a distinguished scholar. To the church and government of his country it was the loss of an enlightened and capable administrator. To Christians of all lands it was the loss of a leader of wisdom and enthusiasm in the cause of church unity. To men of many lands, of all communions and of no communion, it was the loss of a trusted and inspiring friend.

After a brilliant record as a student in Upsala Söderblom went to Paris as pastor of the Swedish church in the French capital. While serving in that capacity he found time to study at the university and was awarded the degree of Doctor of Theology by the evangelical faculty of the Sorbonne in 1901. The same year he was called to a professorship in his own university. While holding this position he lectured in Paris for longer periods and also held a regular appointment in Leipzig. Ultimately he became pro-chancellor of Upsala. He made notable contributions to the literature of his subjects. He was a musician, an organist, especially conversant with Bach.

It was not without inner conflict that, approaching middle life, at the urgency of a liberal element among his clerical colleagues, with the enthusiastic support of the university and at the request of the king, he gave up his career and took the high office of the head of the established church of his country. In the issue it became clear that he had not given up a life devoted to scholarship, but, with his abounding energy, had merely added another life devoted to the religion of Sweden and, as it came to be realized, to the religious interests of the world. No man of our time was more truly an international figure.

It will be remembered that in 1924 he came to this country under commission of his church and in the interest of all the religious communities of Swedish descent in America, both Lutherans and those of the free churches. This task was one which of another man would have demanded great tact. Of Söderblom it demanded only the expression of his generous heart. It entailed long journeys and constant speaking. There was, moreover, another side of it. It would have been impossible for him to visit this country without renewing old contacts and making new ones with institutions of learning throughout the land. He lectured and preached in college chapels, was entertained and entertained. To this work also he gave himself without stint. He returned with a knowledge of our country and a judgement concerning certain of its interests not often equalled.

He had been from the beginning one of the proponents of the International Congress for the History of Religions. He had presided at Oxford over its last sessions before the War. When it came to the question of the resumption of its work after the War, he was again among the most eager. It was decided, in compliment to him, that the resumption of these labours in August, 1929, should take place at the University of Lund. He was, however, already so gravely ill that he was unable to attend. There was scarcely a mention of his name which did not call forth an expression of honour and affection. Equally at Marburg in September, when the four hundredth anniversary of the famous Gespräch was celebrated, Söderblom was to have been one of the great figures. Here too the shadow as of the beginning of the end of a great career was felt by all.

This little book which Mr. Pamp here presents in

translation appeared in its first edition in 1903 in connection with a particular phase of a controversy which most people will remember as a struggle for the recognition of the principles of the so-called higher, that is, the literary and historical criticism of the Scriptures. This particular conflict—nicknamed the Babel-Bible controversy—touching some results of Assyriological studies, was to Söderblom no more than a point of departure. What interested him was not this or any other negation. His aim was to set forth a view of the nature of revelation, the specific quality of the religions of revelation, a view which could be sustained in reason, by history, and in religious experience. It was this constructive portion of the book which drew attention from the beginning. The oft-demanded and long-deferred second edition did not appear until 1930. His preface to this second edition, which the translator has included, lets us into the working of the author's mind. He had deferred issuance because he had intended to make the earlier publication the basis of a more extended work. He had written two other papers upon closely related themes. These he intended to incorporate. By 1930, however, he must have known that he would never be able to carry out this plan. He therefore makes only the most necessary changes in the original article and adds the two supplementary chapters for this second edition.

The translator, a former pupil, is of Swedish extraction, who took his degree as Master of Theology in Harvard University in 1929. He is more widely versed than most in Scandinavian theology and philosophy, a vein of thought to which Söderblom often lovingly refers. Into the translation goes indeed a loyalty to a great man which I also share.

I am convinced that this is a work of high importance to those who would give account to themselves of their own religious convictions or who would have a share in the shaping of an adequate theology.

EDWARD CALDWELL MOORE.

Cambridge, Mass.
  August 1st, 1932.

A S ONE of the foremost leaders in the movement
for unity of the churches and world peace, the
late Archbishop of Sweden, Nathan Söderblom, was
known and honoured throughout the world. Dr. A.
E. Garvie, on hearing of Söderblom's death, said of
him, that he was "the outstanding example of a Pan-
Christian," and added: "If it were possible for the
Protestants to have a pope, Dr. Söderblom would
qualify for that position." The Ecumenical Confer-
ence on Life and Work, held in Stockholm in 1925,
was brought about chiefly by his efforts. His labours
for world peace won for him the Nobel prize, an
award which had universal approval.

Long before this recognition of his eminent place
in the fields of church unity and world peace, Söderblom had won fame as a scholar in the science of religion. For years he occupied chairs in this discipline
in the universities of Upsala and Leipzig and lectured at the foremost universities of Europe. In this
field he has made notable contributions.

It was, however, not only within this specialized

area of thought that he exerted a wide and commanding authority. In his own country he stimulated theological thinking, so that a specifically Swedish school of theology has arisen there since the turn of the century. Swedish thinkers such as Gustaf Aulèn, A. Nygren and others have attracted attention in Europe and their writings are translated into English, Dutch and German. These theologians all acknowledge their debt to Söderblom. He was not a systematic theologian but has contributed to theology by his stimulating discussion of the idea of Revelation.

Aside from articles in Hastings's *Dictionary of Religion and Ethics* and his books, *Christian Fellowship* (Fleming H. Revell Co., Chicago, 1923), and *The Living God* (Oxford University Press, 1933) very little of Söderblom's writings has been available in English. The book herewith presented has not hitherto appeared in any other language than Swedish. Its title in the original is *Uppenbarelsereligion,* literally, "Revealed Religion." It consists of an article written for a "Festskrift" presented to a Swedish scholar in 1903, which constitutes the first chapter of the book, to which the author has added two additional chapters further to elucidate the theme. This little book has become a classic in Swedish theology. It embodies the conviction of Söderblom, that the scientific study of religion will yield an assured knowledge of God. It is said, that on his death-bed he exclaimed: "There is a living God. I can prove it by the history of religion."

That the subject of this book is a timely one is evidenced by the many volumes now being published relating to the theme. The contribution of so noted a scholar as Dr. Söderblom is of the highest value. Interest in his philosophical and theological views is further stimulated by the fact that he was invited to deliver the Gifford Lectures in Edinburgh for 1930-32. He had given the first series before his untimely death in July, 1931.

The introductory pages of the book herewith translated are concerned with the discussion provoked by Professor Friedrich Delitzsch's book, *Babel-und-Bibel,* which at the time when Dr. Söderblom wrote his article was at its height. As this has no vital interest for us today, it has been deemed best to exclude this matter.

The translator was privileged to receive for this rendering a copy of Dr. Söderblom's book in which he had made with his own hand a number of changes and also included additional material. This will explain the differences in the text which may be noted by those familiar with the Swedish original.

Grateful acknowledgement is hereby made to Professor Edward Caldwell Moore for his keen interest in the work of translating Dr. Söderblom's book and for the criticism and suggestions he has offered, which have been of invaluable aid.

FREDERIC E. PAMP.

Boston, Mass.

August 1st, 1932.

Preface

THE little book, "The Nature of Revelation,"
(Uppenbarelsereligion), has for many years
been out of print. There has been much demand for
it and I have often been requested to issue a new edition. I have delayed doing so because I intended to
include its essential contents in some work of larger
dimensions. It has, however, been urged, rightfully I
think, that the book as originally written had gained
a significance for the study of the history of religion
and ought therefore to be made available with as
little change as possible. It is herewith presented in a
revised edition. I have made a few improvements and
minor changes. To the original article have been
added two of later date, which treat of the same subject from different points of view.

NATHAN SÖDERBLOM.

September 24, 1930.

Contents

I

The Religion of Revelation

Some Points of View

I

IN THE discussion as to the merits of different religions and the superiority of one to another, the common standard has been the ethical. One religion is superior to another because it has a better ethical code. In such a comparison the religion of Israel has nothing to fear. It is not, however, by its ethical elevation that a religion is proved superior, although a higher moral code will ultimately be found to accompany that which constitutes the essential superiority of a religion. A comparison of the ethical content of one religion with another cannot give a true *religious* valuation. Religion is not a "thou shalt," and its value is not to be measured by the development which it has reached in ethical relations between man and man. On the contrary, in religion we seek help and life. What does it profit a man if he possess the most excellent worldly wisdom and knowledge of human nature, the best ethical code, yes, even the most beautiful ideals, if faith and hope collapse, if heaven is closed and the spiritual sun of divine power and love is darkened, so that the spirit is left cold and empty? A lofty, severe and sensitive morality, without religion, beautiful and admirable though it may be, is nevertheless nothing but poverty. In comparison with it, however, religion without morality is a shameless pretension, riches which the holder does not possess. The human soul cannot live on morality alone. It must have religion, it must have faith. Harald Höffding in his philosophy of religion has sought to reduce to lowest terms that support for life which man seeks in religion. He has certainly carried the reduction to a minimum when he holds that religion is faith in the persistence of values. But even in this minimum definition, which is evidently inspired by the theory of the conservation of energy and which offers less than the least possible, rather than the reverse, there is contained this truth, that the value of a religion is measured by its ability to give victorious confidence, to guarantee value and meaning to life if this be lived in accordance with its truth. No comparison of moral injunctions can give a true valuation of the religions with which they are historically more or less associated.

Most certainly we must take morals into account in the study and valuation of a religion, and this in two respects. First, with respect to the character of the morals. Second, and this is more fundamental, with respect to the nature of the connection which the religion in question has with the moral life. First and last a religion must be judged by its religious resources. It is impossible to understand the religion of Israel and to see its place in the history of religion without taking the religious point of view. In the nature of things, it is self-evident that the ultimate valuation must be upon the question of the religious power possessed by a religion. This truth has certainly not been accepted and applied in our day. The traditional and, on the whole, undisputed principle is to make the ethical the decisive standard in the history of religions, and to arrange and value religions according to their moral code. No one would dispute the tremendous significance of this principle and its close connection with the question of religious power. But it is not the point of view of religion itself. For the final question put to religion is not:

"How will you shape my life, what ought my life to be?" It is rather this: "How can you rescue my life and sustain it, so that I may not be engulfed in a meaningless existence or lost in despair?" The latter question cannot, however, be separated from the former.

Eduard Geismar has uttered a timely word, not without a pointed paradox which I would include, when he wrote concerning Old Testament religion: "Let it remain there, that element of egoism; therein lies the elevating power of revelation. The strength of Israel is not in an exalted morality; its strength is in its religion, in its faith. There is no greater misrepresentation of the history of Israel than to force it into the modern conception of religion in which religion must be an appendix to morals."

Do morals then lie deeper in human life than religion, so that religion must be based on morals if it is to secure an essential place in life at all? Is morality the only certain thing in the spiritual world, so that religion must draw the certainty of its reality from morals, if it is to have any such at all? It is a persistent, but nevertheless a mistaken conception, that the roots of morality go deeper down and spread more widely in human life than the roots of religion.

Religion stands by itself both in history and in the life of the soul. If anything can be said to have been established by scientific enquiry concerning religion in the past century it is the insight that the ground and nature of religion can as little be satisfactorily explained by locating it in the will as by locating it in the intellect, although it must find expression both in the will and intellect. Neither can it be explained, in the customary triple division of the faculties of man into intellect, will and emotion, by referring it to the emotions, although its role in the emotional life is an exceedingly important one. The roots of religion lie deeper, in its own central organ in man, in the spirit. Pascal calls this centre "the heart." Schleiermacher made the matter clear in his *Reden*. He reveals that the place where religion lives its own and essential life, is in the very innermost centre of the personal life of the individual, where the divine and eternal life is mirrored in a fountain which lies in the deepest depths of the soul, if only that mirror is undimmed. The same experience and insight, which in the science of religion is bound up with the name of Schleiermacher, is found on closer examination, under different terms and in spite of great differences, in all the great and earnest thinkers concerning religion, not only within but also outside of the Biblical religions. The centre of religion in the life of the human being is in the spirit. Man is, according to Rudolph Eucken, the meeting-place of different sorts and degrees of reality.

II

If we compare Babel and Bible from the religious point of view, there is apparent a difference between them, which becomes more marked and assumes a more comprehensive importance as we view the history of religion as a whole. This difference can perhaps best be expressed by making a distinction between nature-religion and culture-religion, on the one hand, and prophetic religion on the other. The uniqueness of the prophetic religion I would characterize by giving it the name of revealed religion.

The two terms, revealed religion and culture-religion require an explanation before we enter upon a discussion of the difference which I have indicated.

1. The word "revelation" is used in this connection in a special sense. A revelation of God is present wherever a real religion is found. Where God is known, it may be even imperfectly and through a

distorting medium, there he has in some degree allowed himself to become known, yes, made himself known. The two other interpretations generally offered, to explain the fact of the existence of religious faith and truth outside the Biblical revelation, break down completely. Are all cases of piety and virtue outside the Christian revelation simply a work of the devil, a caricature perpetrated by demons, as we may read in Augustine? How then can they be true, and in important respects exactly like those of the Christian faith? Muhammed believed that the Jinns by stealth were able to snatch up what was said in heaven. (The Koran, 37:7 ff. and other passages.) Or, if the truth about God, which is found in the religions apart from those of the Bible, be the product of man's own reason, as has been taught all the way from the Apologists of the early church down to the various theories of "natural religion," where shall we draw the line between the divine and the human in the religions of the Bible? Justin, with his sympathy for Greek philosophy and his doctrine of the "logos spermatikos," the Divine Word, sown as a seed (sperma) throughout humanity, and Tatian, proud of being a barbarian and despising the Greeks, represent two constant lines of thought in Christian apologetics. Could the same faith in divine providence, the same religious seriousness and pious practical wisdom in Socrates, or Seneca, or Epictetus be a devilish deception or a self-discovered wisdom, but a work of God in the Psalmist or in Paul or Tertullian? Nay, belief in a general revelation of God is forced upon us, so soon as we make a serious acquaintance with non-Christian religion, even where this shows itself debased, degraded or "ignorant," (Eph. 4:18), and however loudly it may call for the gospel of the Cross. Ultimately all certainty of God and divine matters has its source in an intuitive sense of God. We must concede that Troeltsch and Gunkel and all the younger theologians are right when they demand that we take seriously faith in a general revelation of God. *No religion is a product of culture,* all religion depends on a revelation.

This is an ancient Christian idea. Partly because of the exclusively theological point of view which has characterized different lines of thought in the past century, and partly because of our lack of acquaintance with the literature and spiritual treasures of the ancient world, we have lost some of the fresh, immediate and uplifting feeling, so strong in our older theologians, that it was the same God, our God, who held Socrates "on the watch-tower, where we have been set and which we ought never of our own will to leave," firm against the temptation of suicide; that it was the same God, who met Seneca, "wherever he turned," of whom he knew that "he sustained all things," and that "he is not worshipped with the fattened carcasses of slaughtered oxen nor with gold and silver nor with money which is cast into the treasury, but with a pious and sincere will," and with prayer; "Pray for a sincere heart, for the health of the soul first and then of the body, pray to God with boldness." It was the same God, our God, who gave to Epictetus his strong, humble confidence: "Just that which happens I choose as best; I am satisfied with my fate; for I consider that which God wills better than that which I will. To him I would bind myself in love as a good servant and a faithful slave; his wish, his desire shall be mine; in short, his will be mine!" If this feeling were alive now, we should find sympathy even in ecclesiastical circles with the prayer of Nebuchadnezzar to Marduk:

"A ruler who wishes to obey Thee am I; the work of Thy hands am I.
It is Thou, who has created me, and
Thou hast entrusted to me the lordship over humanity,

According to the mercy, which Thou dost show to all.
Grant that I may love Thy high guidance!
Implant in my heart fear of Thy Divinity!
Grant to me what seemeth good to Thee, for it is Thou
  who hast the lordship over my life.—"

or with the plaintive cry to Ishtar:

"I, Thy servant, pray with sighs unto Thee,
Thou, who dost hear the earnest prayer of the sinner,
Thou, whose glance giveth man life.
O, Thou Almighty one, Queen of the nations,
Thou, the merciful One, who doth turn in mercy and
  receivest the petitions of those who pray."

Enthusiasm for the elevated and powerful elements found in the Babylonian and Assyrian expressions of piety constitutes a reaction against that narrow view which has gone with the over-valuation of the truth-content of the Biblical revelation, such as has been prevalent during the past century. Even pagans have known that "we are also his offspring." They have been "feeling after Him." And "He has not let Himself be without witness." We ought to read Origen's interpretation of such texts. It is high time in this age of world missions and world communications and the final flow of world history in one deep stream, that the Church acquaint itself with the thought of the general revelation of God.

2. This is one side of the matter. On the other side we note that every higher religion demands as a necessary condition a certain measure of culture. This includes the religion of prophecy. No phenomenon in the history of religions, no revelation has sprung forth as a *Deus ex machina* without the given cultural conditions. We shall return to this theme later, and discuss it in greater detail.

The terms culture and revelation cannot, however, be conceived as mutually exclusive. In the area of history there are, generally speaking, no forces or movements which are totally exclusive. But this does not mean that we must not rightfully and necessarily distinguish the different nuances which emerge in history.

This brings us to the principal and most significant distinction which the history of religion has to present. This distinction is not one that cuts sharply across the threads of development where a new woof in the weaving begins. Rather it is a cut lengthwise along the warping of the weave. This distinction reaches back as far as we can see anything clearly in the history of Israel from the time of Moses, but it includes also certain phenomena outside the limits of Israel.

In the first attempt to construct a philosophy of the history of religion, on the basis of a richer and more complete knowledge of this history, C. P. Tiele has set up "the law of the spiritual unity of man" and applied it to the relation of the religious development to that of the general culture. This principle is in so far true that a higher culture cannot in the long run fail to influence religion. But if we mean thereby that the general development of the spirit of man in culture, in the conquest of nature, in social structure, in science, art and morals is matched by that of its religion, so that the higher religion follows the higher culture, religion and general culture appearing side by side in their progress through their different epochs and principal forms, the principle will not hold good. Or rather, it divides the history of religion into two unequal parts, one of which corroborates the law of the spiritual unity of the race, and the other radically contradicts that law.

Let us take a hurried view of that part of the history of religions which is by far the largest, but has least content. I do not now take into account the dim origins, nor even those anticipations of pre-animistic conceptions which are visible among races lowest in the scale. We see at once, however, how the general cultural development, with all that belongs to it, marks the clear, characteristic steps in the advance of religious development. Clan religion, tribal religion, racial religion, all are named from the stages of social construction. Agriculture with its settled habitation becomes of the greatest significance for religion. Several villages and areas are united in larger units. Through a very complicated process, which naturally presents a different appearance at different points but is in reality one process, the gods of a religion are by unification and exclusion gathered into a divine state, ordered according to the different areas of life. Polytheism, which arose with racial religion, is a late phenomenon in the history of religion and proves itself to be a step upward, co-ordinate with political and cultural development, bringing with it order and a richer religious content, greater spiritual power and security, compared with the narrower religious horizon of the tribes and separate localities.

A single observation is sufficient to reveal this. According to ancient thought the god is Lord only within his own territory; only there is he at home and able to aid. When Benhadad and his Syrians were defeated by Ahab, "the servants of the king of Syria said unto him, Their god is a god of the hills; therefore they were stronger than we; but let us fight against them on the plain, and surely we shall be stronger than they." (1 Kings 20:23.)

In order to gain greater and more comprehensive divine protection, it therefore becomes necessary if possible to enrich religion with more gods and thus gradually form a pantheon, if the means and the opportunity are at hand.

A modest beginning of a pantheon was made in Israel by the new and powerful dynasty, which came to the throne with Omri. His son Ahab (911–889 B.C.) married a Tyrian princess. He built a splendid temple to Melkart, the Tyrian Baal, in the new residential city of Samaria itself, and provided it with a staff of prophets. He did not in the least mean to drive out Jahve. In the names of his children the name of Jahve appears in its shorter form. He humbled himself before Elijah, Jahve's prophet. But for political reasons and also for religious reasons, which can easily be imagined, he adopted, in connection with an alliance and closer contact with Tyre, its national god—in keeping with the progress of all religions of antiquity. Then arose a strange, powerful figure, rough and unyielding as granite. Elijah knew that Jahve could tolerate no one at his side. Jahve was a deity, hostile and zealous against other gods.

In Judah they went further. With an open eye for the need of the times and the ruling desire, Ahas (741–726 B.C.) established in a room in the palace a cult of the heavenly bodies according to the Assyrian-Babylonian model. Manasse (696–641 B.C.) moved the images into the temple. Never in the kingdom of Judah has religious zeal in conjunction with politics cultivated and adopted so many ancient Canaanitish or absolutely foreign rites as during the reign of Manasse and of Ammon (641–639 B.C.). Ezekiel tells us what he saw in the temple and beside it in Jerusalem (Ch. 8). Should not the Jerusalem temple provide itself with a pantheon just as all other shrines which kept up with the progress of the age? The temple was in a way to become a polytheistic metropolitan sanctuary. When the temple at Jerusalem of this time was able to compete with the proud shrines of foreign lands in the variety of its equipment, in richness of cult and in the cruel, sacrificial and emotionally charged demands, it was considered a step forward. We must not forget that polytheism, in its own field, is a step forward in religion, even though it was a vile thing in the eyes of the prophets, the champions of genuine Mosaism. To their contemporaries these prophets seemed hopelessly callous and godless, just as the early Christians for the piety of antiquity were *Atheoi,* atheists, because of the provoking simplicity and spirituality of their faith and cult. Nevertheless, when the prophets declared open warfare on the party of progress in religion, they served the cause of religion in the future.

When the religion of race and state, with its polytheism was established, the uniform movement of culture and religion did not cease. Skill in the arts and architecture created within the religions images of the gods and temples. The images grew in magnitude in Egypt and Mesopotamia, or in richness of inventive genius in design and perhaps fantastic fullness of expression in India, or in noble human form among the Greeks. For the watering of the earth and for the needs of agriculture and of commerce on the sea, observations and computations were made of the movements of the stellar bodies and of the changes of the seasons. Theology made use of these advances. Conceptions about the gods and their worship absorbed more and more of the higher ethical elements together with a parallel progress in social ethics. The more complicated and refined mode of life reacted upon religion.

Polytheism is not the last word of culture-religion. Even the divine state at times becomes strongly monarchical in order. Partly because of political reasons, as in the case of Marduk, Ashur, Ammon and Jupiter, or for other reasons, as with Zeus and Indra, one god becomes lord or ruler over the rest. Strong expression of pious zeal in the worship of divine power is found in all stages of polytheism and must not be confused with the tendency to unite the gods as forms of one single deity or as the name of the unfathomable being behind heaven and earth.

Individual approaches toward monotheism in the area of nature-religions and polytheism have never succeeded. In the reign of Rammannirari III in Assyria (811–783 B.C.) it seems that a governor of Kalah and other provinces wished to make Nabu the only god. To please the king and his mother, who probably was a Babylonian princess, he dedicated eight images to Nabu, the deity of Borsippa, Babylon's neighbouring city, with inscriptions which called upon the people to put their trust in this god and in none other. In the year 807 B.C. a splendid temple was erected to Nabu in Kalah.[1]

Still more comprehensive and important is the attempt in Egypt of Huen-Aten, Amenhotep IV, during the 18th dynasty to break with the old religious tradition and worship the disk of the sun, Aten-Ra, alone as god. It can be questioned whether such a monotheism, in which a nature god carries the whole cult and faith, really meant progress. The undertaking was at all events doomed to failure. All that resulted was a unique episode to which the discoveries at El-Amarna, where the religion-reforming Pharaoh built himself a new capital, bear eloquent testimony. A prince in Texcuco in old Mexico, Netzalcuatl, is said to have worshipped one divinity without images and without bloody sacrifices. Something similar is related of a prince of the Incas in Peru, Tupak Yupomki. Neither succeeded in carrying out his plans of reform.

To parallel such "monotheism," depending on the will, either of an enlightened or of a capricious ruler, with Jahve-monotheism,[2] is to misunderstand

---

[1] C. P. Tiele, *Geschiedenis*, I. 178.
[2] H. Winckler, *Abraham als Babylonier, Joseph als Ägypter*, 31 ff.

the clear story of the history of religion. No nature-god or culture-god has ever been able to achieve a real monotheism of universal or spiritual nature. For this achievement there was demanded the revelation of the prophets.

In the exercise of thought the powers of speculation and abstraction are trained and logical demands are sharpened. In India there enters with the Upanishads a new period for religion in connection with a view of the phenomenality of the world. The subtlety of mind and the consistency of thought shown in the carrying of this thought into abstract idealism and acosmism is in no sense inferior to similar later operations of thought in Greece and in modern times.

Among peoples noted for intellectual acumen, chiefly those of India and Persia, this aspect of culture has brought new epochs for religion. With the spiritualizing of the conception of God followed the vanishing of the figures of the gods. The Eternal Being of Brahmanism became finally so emptied of religious content that at least one of the many teachers of salvation and organizers of orders, Gautama Buddha, did away with this figure entirely. It had become an insufferable weight, a burden to

the seeker of salvation. None, I emphasize, none of
the polytheistic gods, the gods which in accordance
with the law of the spiritual unity of man, have followed the development of culture, has in the long
run been able to endure the rarefied atmosphere of
the highest elevations of spiritual culture. Not one.
The living divine beings have faded away or have
been lost in "the Great Unknown." They have become wrapped in "the sacred twilight" or have been
swallowed up in "the divine darkness."

We can trace clearly the development into polytheism, monarchic supremacy, and from thence out
into pantheism, idealism, acosmism or religious ag-
nosticism. The figures of the gods of nature-religion
and culture-religion emerge out of prehistoric shadows in fantastic, shapeless animal phantoms, which
then take on form, order, refinement, human qualities, and then these numerous, but not innumerable
throngs march past us, well-defined forms indeed.
They continue their march and are lost in the eve-
ning shadows on the horizon. Culture is doomed to
fail and wither away, or commit suicide in the philosophical conclusion that labour is in vain and culture itself without meaning, unless it is borne up by

a strong and vital religious faith.[1] The religion which merely accompanies this cultural development, without infusing new elements of revelation, shares its fate. Is China an exception? No, Laotse's "tao" has very little left of a living deity. In the religion of the state, the ethical reform of Confucius left a minimum of divine worship for the sake of the community. Reasons of state and reverence for authority have been stronger than the spiritual demands of culture. Pagan Rome, in its way, might have become a counterpart, had it but survived.

The second great world-historic development belongs, if we except Eastern Asia, to the Semitic and the Indo-germanic peoples. Two ancient folk-gods have there been able to maintain themselves, Ahura-Mazda and Jahve, an Aryan and a Semitic folk-god. But this has been possible just because and only because something other than cultural religion, something new, has there emerged. Because of a new prophetic content these gods have escaped the fate of those of the culture-religions,

---

[1] Cf. V. Norström, *Vad vi behöva, Radikalism ännu en gång,* etc. Also, R. Eucken's *Der Wahrheitsgehalt der Religion.* (Eng. *The Truth of Religion.*)

even though Ahura-Mazda later tended more toward polytheism than did the Mosaic revealed religion in Israel or did the gospel still later in the Church.

The dissolution of polytheism by the higher intellectual and moral culture into pantheism and idealism does not mean the destruction of all personal divine beings. For this development did not penetrate to the masses. Folk-religion demands a living Deity. New gods spring up. Buddhism procured itself many such Buddhas and Budhisatvas without any warrant being found for them in the writings or claims of Buddha himself. Of all sects and religions, which without contact with revealed religion, have grown up on a soil that had been prepared by the higher intellectual culture in India and the Ancient world, two, namely Krishnaism in India and Mithraism in the Roman world, have shown a remarkable power to make vivid the certainty of the comforting nearness and living presence of their deities in a way that has given to these a characteristic difference from the ancient national divinities. Both Krishna and Mithra are equipped with human experiences and human achievements in a way different from that with which the myths have related the story of the polytheistic gods. To them has been joined a bit of invented salvation story. That kind of Jesus-worship, which is called "evangelism," although this name hardly fits, because it lacks the moral salt of the evangel and the purification of personality which constitutes the uniqueness of historical revealed religion, often reveals in its language and terms of expression a striking similarity to these and other cults from the later culture of India and the Ancient world. They are so similar that the name of Krishna or of Mithra or of some other can be substituted for the name of Jesus. But monotheistic these cults are not. Their mediators cannot by any power of the imagination or by condensation of religious emotion and tradition be changed into that which no human operation, after all, can establish, a historic revelation of the Divine.

Culture and religion accompany each other, as we have seen, although with disparateness and unevenness. The road leads to polytheism, and then farther on, away again from polytheism, to unity, but never to a real, monotheistic, universal faith in the living God.

The exceptions are easily counted. The more sharply do they stand out. Zoroaster's Ahura-Mazda was fundamentally monotheistic. He is not a tribal god beside others. The Daevas are combated not as gods but as devils. He is not the highest in a pantheon of nature gods. In the Gathas he is surrounded by celestial servants, not rivals. No divine figure outside the Bible approaches him in spirituality and monotheistic exaltation. And what about the culture? The reform of Zoroaster was not only a religious but an economic reform, one of the primitive among these. It marks the transition from the life of hunting and nomadic habits to that of settled dwellings and ordered labour in field and pasture. The great cultural nations, however, have not been able to bring forth a conception of God such as Zoroaster's, even on the higher levels of civilization, when they had left this transition so far in the dim past that it had faded from memory.

Still more striking is the difference in the relation which the prophetic religion of Israel bore to general culture. The recently unified tribes came as barbaric conquerors into contact with the Canaanitish culture, which for one or more millenniums had been saturated with Babylonian civilization. This higher culture with agriculture, vineyards and city life, they gradually acquired. And yet, after a long period of the monarchy had elapsed, the powerful, genuine Mosaism rises again in league with nomadic life against the higher development of tilling the soil, planting vineyards and building cities, with all the accompanying advantages. It is a pity that H. S. Vodskov never gave us the second volume of his great work on *Sjeledyrkelse og Naturdyrkelse,* (Worship of Souls and Worship of Nature). In this book, although only a fragment, through which he made himself a never-fading name among Scandinavian scholars, he makes the following daring statement. "Man, at the higher hunting and nomadic stage is inferior to the civilized man in all material arts and achievements, but he is just as much superior to him in religion, language and social structure." (p. lxiv.) He gives as an example from religions, the worship of souls. This never gained the power in nomadic life which it did in the settled state. Vodskov's statement is a direct contradiction of the law of the spiritual unity of mankind. But is it true in a general application? It is true, if what one means is, that *one nomadic* people attained among the religions of the world a greater importance than all agricultural peoples combined. The higher, prophetic religion asserts itself even in com-

pany with a lower level of culture, yes, even in antago-
nism to a higher civilization. Budde points out that it
was fortunate that the Rechabites, who were Mosa-
ists inimical to civilization, did not gain the victory,
for Jehovah became the giver and Lord of the higher
civilization as well. Thereby the older Jahveism was
freed from that austerity, which is so repelling and
inhuman to us. But if we ask whence that element
had its origin which has been so fruitful and indispensable for the religious life of humanity, from
nomadic Mosaism, or from the settled life under
Canaanitish influence, when Jahve acquired the
characteristics of the culture gods without losing his
identity, the answer cannot be uncertain. It was
through Moses that the religion of Jahve was hin-
dered from pursuing the usual course of culture-
religion. The trend toward polytheism was stopped
in spite of natural tendencies and efforts, and the
Jahve religion was prevented from dissolving into
pantheism and idealism. The highest spiritual and
ethical conception of God in the Gospel only serves
to bring Him closer and make Him more living
than ever. Perhaps it was earlier even than Moses.
The Old Testament knows of no special revelation
to Abraham. (Cf. Kittel, *Geschichte des Volkes*

Israel.) Attempts to determine historically what is
the contribution of Abraham to religion have, hitherto at least, proved unsatisfying, for the reason,
among others, that they prove too much or must deal
with only general and formless conceptions. This is
true even of such attempts to bring to light an Abra-
hamic religion which resolutely take their stand on
scientific grounds, as that of A. Klostermann, who attempts to vindicate in his *Geschichte des Volkes Israel*
a "spiritual, personal character" for the "peculiar religion of Abraham." Up to the time of Moses, religion seems not yet to have reached the cross-roads,
where the road to polytheism and "the divine" ab-
stractions leads off from the way to the living God,
never to meet it again. Have we the right to expect
information about Abraham in the cuneiform inscriptions, or at least such information as will permit conclusions and well-based combinations concerning the religion of Abraham? Hugo Winkler
writes: "These documents are official writings and
one cannot expect of them, that those matters should
have importance for them, which the course of history has shown to be determining in the development of the world. The importance, for example,
that Kant has won for the spiritual life of the

modern world, cannot be discovered from the state archives of his own time. Humanity has not been able within the short span of a generation to recognize the importance of the life work of its leading personalities." However, the certainty with which Assyriological research has moved in the vast distances of the past,—vast, and yet in comparison with the existence of the race so insignificant, has taken away something of the sceptical fear, which, without further discussion, considered it unscientific to hold the patriarchs to be what tradition with one voice proclaims them, historical personalities. Even though it be precarious to seek in the time of Abraham an epoch of radical importance for the religion of Israel, —the importance for religion that Abraham later won as "the father of the faithful" is another matter,—yet it is impossible to place the epoch-making element in revealed religion *after* the time of Moses. To quote J. W. Rothstein, "One must finally, with Reuss, allow it to stand, that the foundation of the religious development of the Old Testament was laid where, according to the Biblical tradition it was laid, in the time of Moses and through Moses." The great prophets, an Amos, a Hosea, an Isaiah, a Jeremiah, the psalmist Ebed-Jahve, the author of the 73d Psalm,

sometimes reveal in religious faith and morals an
elevation which even the twentieth Christian century
has not been able to attain. The distance between them
and the most beautiful examples of Babylonian documents quoted by Delitzsch is as the distance between
heaven and earth.[1] They move on a different, a
higher plane. It is self-evident, it verges almost upon
a truism, to note the fact, that in the degree in which
the prophetic faith of Israel rises above the religion of
Babylon, by just so much does the general culture of
Babylon, the spiritual capital, the *ville lumière* of its
day, with its science, its art, its social development
and its ancient history, rise above Israel, that queer
upstart on the banks of the Jordan. The redemption
of the world, the unconquerable certainty of faith in
the loving will of the living God based on Jesus
Christ, after all has not come from Babylon, or
Athens, or Rome, but from Galilee and Jerusalem.

Of course, it is possible to find the prophetic religion in the guise of a culture-religion, accompanied
by the higher humanities and intellectual life of the
times. To find this, one must go to the Hellenistic
Judaism of the Diaspora and to Christianity, when

---

[1] Cf. H. Gunkel, *Israel und Babylonien*, p. 37 f.

it had robed itself in the rich spiritual garments of antiquity. But if this dazzling sight deceives us and produces the illusion that the secret of the triumphant advance of Christianity was Greek philosophy, art, science and social power, history abundantly proves, that the power and the victory came rather from the Gospel and the prophetic movement, poor in culture, but not hostile to culture, nor deficient in culture. Jesus does not belong to the history of cultural religion. Jesus, the fulfiller of Moses and the prophets, did not come to establish a new religion, but rather to do away with all religions and establish the Kingdom of God. A religion with all the characteristics of such has risen out of his legacy. But this is only a transition, a means toward the end, the Kingdom of God. It is not yet made manifest what we shall be.

The religion of the prophets is not a stage in the development of religion, but a phenomenon by itself. Attempts to make it the product of the development of national religion, fascinating as they may be, are contrary to the actual records of the history of religions. The influence of great personalities on religion we note in many places. They concentrate in the period from the eighth to the sixth centuries before Christ, in widely separated lands: Laotse, Confucius, Zoroaster, Buddha, the literary prophets of Israel and the earlier Greek teachers of redemptive religion. But did these come with new creative religious ideas? Did they speak in the name of the living God? Confucius was an ethical and social teacher. Laotse had a more speculative and inward quality. But we have already had cause to ask if in his faith there is found any love of a living and active deity. Gautama Buddha released religious blessedness and the way to it from the very idea of God. In Greece not one of the great personalities of the higher and nobler piety was able to express his experience of God in a prophetic proclamation of the rule and living power of God, even though the faith of some, especially of the later Stoics, due to the experience of Socrates, has much of the temper of prophetism. The last and finest religious creation of the Greek spirit, Neo-Platonism, the chief exponent of which, Plotinus, is considered by Augustine to be the best interpreter of Plato, has all the characteristics of polytheism refined into pantheism and idealism, and of spiritualized and ethicized mysticism. With its contemplation and ecstatic union with the "Unspeakable" as the ideal form of piety, this mys-

ticism is both a nature mysticism and a mysticism of
infinity in contrast to the personal mysticism of the
prophetic movement.

There remain the work of Zoroaster and of Moses
and the prophets. The religion of Zoroaster, however, does not count in the main for the history of
religion, owing to its own narrow limitations and to
the fact that it was never fully carried out. There is
something appealing in the thought that the Jewish
piety in contact with the Persian religion recognized
in it something of its own religious faith and was
therefore sensitive to influence from it. The voice of
God spoke of Cyrus through the mouth of the
prophet: "Behold my servant, whom I have chosen."
(Isa. 45.) But it is clear that Cyrus did not have the
reformed Mazda faith. The religious experience and
revelation of God which has been most penetrating
and significant for the religious history of mankind,
the prophetic religion, arises in a very humble cultural surrounding, separated from the stream of the
great, widespread development of society, of ethics, of
culture and thought. Culture has since adopted it,
from it received a new soul, and has been saved from
self-destruction. Although culture has in turn influ-

enced this religion, it has not given to it any new religious power.

This does not mean that the prophets came into history, detached from that which preceded them, outside the cultural continuity. No prophet, no revelation, ever comes before the fulness of time, or until the necessary conditions are at hand. (Mark 1:15; Gal. 4:4.) These conditions are of historical and psychological nature. They are such that they exclude entirely the conception of divine arbitrariness. No hiatus, no leap takes place. The psychological and historical continuity is unbroken. And yet, the religion of the prophets offers for the science of religion, a different and a much more difficult problem than that of nature-religion or culture-religion. It is not solved by simply saying, we do not see the continuity, therefore it must be God's work. This would be a theological subterfuge, as dangerous as it is comfortable, thus to put God in where the continuity is not clear. This is the mode of thought upon which Positivism proceeds when it holds that God is the explanation of all the unknown, and, in the measure that enlightenment spreads its illumination, there is less need of God as an explanation. Not so. The divine is revealed in the human. We cannot discover any gap in the historical and psychological continuity of the life of the prophet. Had we the eyes of God all would lie clearly for us in its continuous process. Neither can we in the prophetic religion draw a line around certain words or certain events and say, here is God and revelation, there is man and Nature. Even in the perfect revelation of God in the person of Christ the divine and the human are commingled, as the theologians have expressed in the doctrine of the *communicatio idiomatum.*

It is not our ignorance nor the obscurity of the problem which mark the divine in the work of the prophets. It is not the difficulty and darkness which surround the origin of the prophetic religion which is the determining element. Rather, it is the clear insight that a new stream of profound religious content, which itself points to an immediate contact with God as its source, has come into the world through the prophets. "Every genius on earth is a puzzle for history. The greatest genius is always the religious genius. Every new creation of genius can be only partially explained by the times. There is always left a remainder, something inexplicable.

The greatest remainder of this sort is always left by the creative religious genius, by him who lays hold more deeply upon the mysterious basis of life." [1] In the prophetic religion there breaks forth a living stream of immediate experience of the divine more powerful than ever appears in culture-religion. This implies, as we shall see, a knowledge of God which is richer than, and in an essential way different from, that which is outside of the prophetic religion. We have already seen that it comes forth in a unique way in the history of religion, in a relative independence of the course of general culture, which discredits completely the law of the spiritual unity of the race, conceived in the manner above pointed out. Far better it would be to postulate for this law in the spiritual history of humanity, a law of the distribution of tasks. This gives the task of culture to some peoples, for example, the Babylonians. Their significance for the history of religion would have been lost in the sands if it had not been for the fact that the prophetic religion of Israel had taken up and re-shaped some elements of the ancient wisdom of this highly cultured people. This law has chosen out

---

[1] R. Kittel, *Der Babel-Bibel-Streit und die Offenbarungsfrage,* page 12. Cf. also *Gestalten und Gedanken in Israel,* by the same author.

one people to be pre-eminently the people of religion
and to build for the future of religion.

"The analogy of members in a body, by which
the apostle Paul, in a manner unsurpassed, describes
the relation in which every individual in a community, with his special vocation and his own talents and gifts, stands to the community itself in its
entirety, can be applied also to nations in respect to
their role and their significance for the great family
of humanity. And, as the life of the body most intimately depends on the proper function of small
organs, the heart, the brain, the lungs, etc., so nations may have a function which does not depend
on their size, their military strength or even upon
their culture and refinement."[1] Since the metaphysical and metahistorical venture of faith has been
made from the awareness and certainty of the divine
to the conception of God, his creation, his self-
impartation, his revelation, it is difficult for one to
avoid clearly distinguishing in the history of religion
a unique revelation, that of the prophetic religion,
the revealed religion, in the course of sacred history
throughout the ages.

But is not the conception of a unique revelation,

---

[1] N. Innell, *Menskliga utvecklingens historia*, II, 345.

of a chosen people of religion, an unworthy one and contrary to the love and justice of God? This ancient objection of Celsus has weight even today. According to him Jews and Christians believed that God had for their sake established the earth and the heavens. He compares the Christians to worms, and pictures them as coming forth and saying: "The heavens God sets aside, and the earth, great as it is, he forsakes, to employ himself only with us and to have relations with us alone. To us he sends messengers constantly and seeks to unite us with himself eternally." (Origen, *Contra Celsum* IV. 27, 28.) I pass by Origen's confutation of Celsus with the Scriptural statements of the all-embracing power and love of God and the universality of redemption. But it is one thing to reckon what God *ought* to have done according to our ideas of Him and His being. It is another thing to investigate so far as is possible for us what He actually *has done* in the life and history of mankind. I see very clearly how fascinating for apologetics is that view of Christianity, which holds that it is the flower of the development of religion, its final end, into which all the different lines of general revelation have converged.

In the world of thought, in a transcendent view of

evolution, Christianity can of course be designated
as the highest stage of development or its end, as
the point where a new species has been formed, a
new life, that of the super-man, the super-human
life, as we Christians say, the divine-human life has
appeared. Apologetics has the full right to claim that
in Christianity we have a higher unity, above the
absorption of Zoroastrianism in culture, above Buddhism's denial of culture, above the theocracy of
Semitic religion and the Theanthropy of the Arians,
above the divine immanence and transcendence. But
historically something else has happened. The land
of Israel was so situated that the prophetic religion
came into contact with other religions and other
civilizations. Through this it received incalculable
material and impulse for the perfecting and the determining of its own unique character through the
re-shaping or else the rejection of this foreign element. Abraham came from Mesopotamia, Joseph
and Moses came from Egypt. In this, according to
Winckler, there lies before us in general contours the
history of a whole culture.[1] In Canaan Israel came

---

[1] *Abraham als Babylonier, Joseph als Ägypter. Der weltgeschichtliche
Hintergrund der biblischen Vätergeschichten auf Grund der Keilin-
schriften dargestellt.*

daily in contact with the native religions. For a century it has been held as certain that belief in resurrection and in a devil came from the Parsees. Certain it is that the Jews learned to know Mazda worship. Later Judaism shows the influence of Hellenism. The rich and significant work of W. Bousset, *Die Religion des Judentums im neutestamentlichen Zeitalter,* has a sixth and final section with the title: "The Problem of the History of Religion," which is summarized as follows: "The progressively unified life of humanity and its religious development drew Judaism more and more powerfully into its stream." "Authenticated influences penetrate into the very centre of its religion." "Not alone a *single* religion has contributed to the origin of Christianity, but contact with the whole of Western civilization, the religions of the Hellenistic period of culture." "Judaism was the crucible into which the different elements were gathered." Such a view in general is not new. It has arisen at different times with different degrees of power, ever since the ancient Christian historical writers attempted to interpret all preceding religions as merely preparations for their own. Bousset has presented this view with scientific authority and consequent balance. But however highly these influences may be valued it is impossible to make of Christianity the *quinta essentia* of all these elements, the peak of the development of religion. In the eighteenth century, as also in our day, a number of books have been published, which have found the source of the religion of Moses in the mysteries of the Egyptian priests or in some cryptic Chaldean wisdom. Now we are able to see more clearly what Israel really did receive from the East. Moses cannot be set in the line of Mesopotamian religions. We know too much for this. We realize that the most valuable element is the *exclusive property of prophetic religion*. Christianity lies before us, not as the end of the journey of religion aided by culture, but *as the full completion of a special revelation of God*.

If we wish to find an open-hearted readiness to absorb everything good and true, one must turn elsewhere than to the prophets and the Gospel, which are nevertheless the gold-producing vein of religion in the world. The ideal of humanity in Hellenism also contained religious elements of significant nature, which came most clearly to light in the immortally beautiful swan song of the Hellenic spirit, neo-Platonism. On its scale every tone of the whole religious development of humanity readily found place—all except Judaism and Christianity, because of their unreasonable demands. Plotinus (d.A.D. 270) would not even mention the land of his birth, according to his biographer, Porphyrios. The biographer of Proclus (d.A.D. 485) tells us that he considered "that it was improper for a philosopher to observe the festive rites of this or that city or state, for he was to be rather the high-priest of the whole world." In the flower of Indian culture we find equally beautiful words of religious tolerance. Krishna says in *Bhagavad-gita,* chap. IX, the Song of Songs of Hindu piety, that if one has a true faith and devotion to other gods, it is faith and devotion to Krishna, although in a wrong way. One is reminded of words of Luther in *The Larger Catechism,* "Only the faith and trust of the heart make either God or idol. If your faith and trust are right and sincere, you have the true God, and conversely, if your faith and trust are false and wrong, you have not the true God; for these two, God and faith belong together and must be joined."

The prophets and the Gospel speak a different language. "No one knoweth the Father except the Son and he to whomsoever the Son willeth to re-

veal him." So far it is true, that "Christianity was in
the fullest sense particularistic and rejected all other
religions, while Hellenism, in the best sense of the
word universalistic, awarded a certain legitimacy to
every form of religion." [1] Christianity felt that it had
something its own and this particularism has proved
to be the strongest religious power in all the world.
For in Christ it possesses that on which, in the death
struggle of the human spirit, everything finally depends, certainty of the living God.

If we view the history of religion, not as progress-
ing in accordance with our scheme of thought, but
from the point of view of what it actually is, we
cannot deny the fact that the interpretation given by
the *Auctor ad Theophilum* of the words of Barna-
bas and Paul, "God suffered all the nations to walk
in their own ways, and yet he left himself not without witness," is more realistic and striking than later
constructions. Certainly the admonition: "Turn to
the living God," marks the difference between revealed or prophetic religion and other religions of
a high type. Sir Alfred C. Lyall in *Asiatic Studies*
closes a review of the religious situation in India

[1] K. H. E. de Jong, "Plutarchus en het antieke Christendom," in
Theologisch Tijdschrift 1903.

with the statement that he is certainly not able to trace the course which imagination and thought has pursued in the progress from belief in millions of gods to the acknowledgement of an all-embracing Spirit and to the insight that he is unknowable. "I can say only, that after long personal observation of religion in India, I have received the impression that the whole marvellous construction has come through what, for want of a better expression, I must call a natural growth." (*Asiatic Studies,* 2 ed. II, 323.)

III

The special relation in which this revealed religion stands to the general development of culture is matched by the inner character which it possesses, which, in comparison with any corresponding religions, marks it as superior not only in degree, but essentially differing from them in those qualities which are common to all religions.

This is shown in the conception of God and of the relation to God. In what follows I am not seeking to make an evaluation, a weighing of higher and lower, but rather I shall seek to show in the most important essentials the vital difference between what I here summarize, *with the restrictions noted above,* under the designations culture-religion and revealed religion. Then, in the final analysis, it will depend upon our own personal attitude in religion to which one we shall award the precedence in its highest and purest expression.

The faith of this revealed religion is directed to *the one, living, spiritual God, who is active in history and there revealed.*

The conception of the unity of God and of his living personality in reality at once excludes the experiences and thoughts of the divine found outside the prophetic religion. Even though other religions may have a conception of God as living and active, comforting and helping, warning and punishing, in other words a conception of God that is filled with religious content, still the deity is not monotheistically conceived in religions outside of the prophetic religion. These are either at such a low stage of tribal religion, or still lower, that there can be no question of monotheism, nor even of polytheism, or else they are at the stage of polytheism, which in the history of religion shows possibilities of some development, but according to the general testimony of facts is exceedingly limited. If a striving toward unity in the conception of God has begun to assert itself, the power to retain step by step the certainty of the living, active love and power of God which awakens trust and fear, is paralysed. At first the divine monarch is elevated above every immediate contact with the world of men, and the chain of intermediary powers is lengthened more and more. Then, on a higher plane of development, the deity disappears into the distant unknown, beyond every positive attribute. Viewed from the standpoint of religion it is perfectly consistent and really a stroke of genius, that Gautama Buddha, when the sublimation had proceeded thus far, realized, with his experience and insight, that such a conception of God is without any value for the satisfaction of human longing for redemption from suffering, and made the purified religious attitude itself, Nirvana, the highest and only end of religion. It is the despairing consequence of nature-religion and culture-religion, which however proved liberating and fructifying for religion.

To be complete we should here make an addition. Within the religion of India there arose, as nearly as we can determine, in the second or third century before Christ, a new doctrine of redemption, which differs radically from the mystic practices and the mysticism of infinity, which had developed either into absorption into the impersonal Brahma or else into the original methodical, self-redemption of Buddhism. I mean the doctrine of Bhakti. In the *Bhagavadgita,* its classical source, in the *Bhaktisutras* and in innumerable later works, is described how salvation is won, not by human effort, but through Bhakti, "devotion," love for a personal deity. We here are concerned not with a historical revelation in a strict sense. This Bhakti redemption has never led to a real monotheism, even though in the moment of communion with the deity, the loving and worshipping soul deals with a single deity conceived as personal. Nevertheless, outside of the boundaries of the prophetic religions and of the Christian Church there is no phenomenon, no doctrine of redemption, which in importance approaches the religion of Bhakti. However, we cannot in this connection do more than make the above suggestions.

What saved the conception of God from fading out of the religion of Jahve and of the Mazda faith? As far as we can ascertain this was due, not to something which emerged in the development, such as a better ethic, a finer spirituality, individualism or universalism, but rather it was due to the nature of the origin of these national religions. It lay in the very fact that they were *founded* religions, i.e., had personal founders.

Whatever may have been the previous history of the Ahura-Mazda religion, it is certain, that before it became the religion of the chief Vistaspa and his people, as he appears in the *Gathas,* and finally the religion of the Persian power, it was the personal religion of Zoroaster. It had gone through the filtration of personal experience and conviction, of a prophetic consciousness of God. His experience of God brought about a radical upheaval, the importance of which can be appreciated only at a distance. Mazda became, not only as did Varuna, the highest of the gods and the guardian of the lawbound order of things (*aša, rta*), but in principle the only God. The other gods were excluded and became evil powers whose worship was forbidden, and his prophet knew that God, through the upheavals of history, would bring about the triumph of his cause, the cause of faith.

Within the higher religious stratum of the Greek civilization there existed a clear consciousness that the religion of Zoroaster possessed something in the direction of a vital knowledge of God, which the

Greeks lacked, in spite of all their varieties of religion and their treasures of culture and their sublime philosophical power and refinement. The rhetorician Dion Chrysostom, of the first and second decade after Christ, is a high example of the monotheistic faith, as true as one could find at the time among the cultured people of the cities. Dion speaks of God as "the wisest and most worthy guide and legislator" and points out that the poets had really called "the chief and greatest god the father and king of all reasonable beings." But when there is question of the government and activity of God, of the "chariot of Zeus," Dion has a sentence to which I would call attention. "But the chariot of the mighty and holy Zeus not one of the poets has worthily celebrated in song, neither Homer nor Hesiod, but on the contrary Zoroaster and the Magi, which have learned of him." There is a feeling that Zoroaster had experienced and understood more of the being of God than the poets and wise men of Hellas.

Among the Jews two corresponding elements appear in the work of Moses with greater potency and a richer and more profound historical vitality, the idea of personality in the conception of God, and the conception of God as the God of history. How

Jahve previously had been known and worshipped is veiled in uncertainty. Will this uncertainty ever be removed? But there is scarcely room for any hesitation in believing that the experience of Moses, the revelation to Moses and through him, was the fundamental thing in the whole future history of the prophetic knowledge and worship of God in its deep differentiation from anything which was developed in the environing religions. "Through Moses Jahve was raised above mere Nature in that he became the covenant God for seven tribes, after he had become for Moses—and here is the most important thing—the God of his life, his rescuer and helper. All of the rich future development of Jahveism above the related religions, from which in the beginning, at least in an outward way it did not differ, has its origin in the person of Moses." [1]

In the first place, Jahve had, through a divine self-revelation become *the God of Moses* in a special sense before He became the God of the covenant he established.[2] In the second place, the power and love

---

[1] C. P. Tiele, *Geschiedenis van den Godsdienst in de Oudheid*, L. pp. 282 f.

[2] This is the meaning of the brilliant distinction which Budde makes, which however hardly can be sustained, between the religion which is *inherited*, and the Jahveism of Moses which was a chosen religion.

of Jahve became known and certified by the redemption out of Egypt. Israel always remembered
and never tired of celebrating the mighty deliverance of God, the extraordinary event in Nature
which forever bound up the new Mosaic knowledge of God in its evidence and origin with the exo-
dus from Egypt. Most wonderful of all, a fact the
significance and wide-reaching effect of which can
scarcely be overestimated, was that Moses saw the
work of God in history. The Babylonian religion
also knew of a divine struggle against the violence
of the sea, the battle of Marduk against the sea
monster Tiamat before he killed the primeval beast
and made the world out of its carcass. Gunkel has
shown [1] that the Babylonian primitive tradition here
and there in the Old Testament raises its head out
of the popular beliefs into the literature, where
otherwise the prophetic reshaping of the creation
story dominates. At times the mythical struggle of
the gods with the sea monster and the deliverance
out of Egypt through the Red Sea are mingled in-
distinctly in the texts. These all are characteristic expressions of the difference between nature-religions
and culture-religions, on the one hand, and the

---

[1] *Schöpfung und Chaos,* 29 ff.

prophetic religion on the other. In nature-religions there is pictured the struggle of the deity against the wild violence of nature, of culture against nature, of order in nature against violence in nature. In the prophetic religion we have related the experience of divine will and purpose in history, the intervention of God at the significant birth of the people as a nation.

Religion has thus received a double foundation of a new kind. God is active in history, not merely in nature and the social order. God is revealed also as the living God in the consciousness of the prophet, not simply sensed as the source of mysterious, infinite power in an ecstatic trance.

The differences between the work of Zoroaster and that of Moses, fraught with such great consequences for the future, come to light, in the very beginning, in the contrasts noted above. The activity of God in history received a powerful and gripping expression for all time in the Jewish faith in God. To this day the deliverance out of Egypt, celebrated in the Psalms, has an important place in the Jewish prayer books. The founder, the prophet, was succeeded by a line of followers through which new streams of constantly enriching impartation and knowledge of God flowed in, so that the history of the religion of

Israel became, not simply a development of the content given in its beginning, but a successive re-creation, culminating and completed in Jesus Christ. There is considerable truth in the well-known saying that, strictly speaking, a religion never becomes anything more than what it was in the beginning. Its history is nothing but a spinning out, a development, a utilization of that which was given in it from the start. This is essentially true of the Mazda religion. But in Israel a new content of revelation comes in through new revealers.

The prophetic religion of Israel has by preference seen the faithfulness, grace and power of God revealed in the deliverance out of Egypt and in the personalities of the men of God, whom He has sent His people. "Also I brought you up out of the land of Egypt, and led you forty years in the wilderness, to possess the land of the Amorite. And I raised up of your sons for prophets and of your young men for Nazarites. Is it not even thus, O ye children of Israel? saith Jehovah." (Amos 2:10 f.) [1] The line of bearers and interpreters of the personal and historical divine revelation is unified into a sacred history, in which the love and righteousness of the living

---

[1] Cf. Hosea 12:13. Jer. 7:13. Deut. 18:15 ff. and other passages.

God is delineated for faith, so that the deity can be called in a proper sense a *revealed God,* not "an unknown God," nor a hidden God. In this sense a historical revelation is possessed by the religion of the Hebrew prophets along and by its heir, Christianity, which sees in Jesus Christ the fulfillment of revelation, "the fulness of the godhead bodily." Therefore it may be called, from the point of view of the history of religions, revealed religion in a special sense. Luther wrote in *De servo arbitrio,* 222:

"Let God in His majesty and being alone. For as such we cannot have anything to do with Him, nor has He wished that we have anything to do with Him as such. But only in the measure that He is clothed and revealed in His word, by which He presents Himself to us do we have anything to do with Him. For the Word is His beauty and glory. The Psalmist praises Him as He is clad in the Word." *"Reliquendus est Deus in maiestate et natura sua, sic enim nihil nos cum illo habemus agere, nec sic voluit a nobis agi cum eo, sed quatenus indutus et proditus est verbo suo, quo nobis sese obtulit, cum eo agimus, quod est decor et gloria eius; quo Psalmista eum celebrat indutum."*

In bringing out this distinction I employ the *historical* point of view, not the *dogmatic.* The latter, much more important for theology, must take for its point of departure the experience which the Church and the individual has of the historical redemption fulfilled in Christ, as a genuine revelation of God. Neither do I here propose the *apologetical* point of view, which makes comparisons and seeks to show the superiority of Christianity. Rather I ask: Are we justified historically in calling the Biblical development of religion revealed religion in a specific sense?

The conception which the prophetic religion has of the work of God in history is revealed in the fact that the religions of Zoroaster and of Moses are the only ones which have developed a complete *eschatology*, with resurrection, world judgement with world restoration and perfection and faith in a moral and religious purpose in the course of world history.[1] Not the proudest nations, not the most ancient and excellent historical writings, not the keenest speculation outside the prophetic religions, has been able to give birth to such a profound conception of the rule of God in the world. This rule of God is sometimes realized gradually, step by step, sometimes at one swift stroke; a conception of divine judgement

[1] Cf. my book, *La Vie future,* ch. IV. (*Annales du Musée Guimet Bibl. d'études,* part IX.)

upon nations and generations, with the conception of the final perfection of the world in a perfect age. Not Rameses, not Hammurabi, not Assurbanipal, not Alexander the Great, not Cæsar, have possessed the power to give such an eschatological horizon to their undertakings. "For the Greeks, as well as for their Latin disciples, the thought of meaning in the eternal struggle, of an end above the victories or defeats of the combatants, is totally wanting." (Harald Hjärne.) Apocalyptic and history, on the whole, had no value for mysticism nor for rationalism. God's work is viewed by mysticism as timeless. Augustine, Bossuet and Hegel have sought to interpret the underlying connection of history, its meaning and its end. But they have not this conception. The philosophy of history has seen the light of day in the despised and misunderstood Jewish apocalyptic and its Parsee equivalent. "Give a man a true apocalyptic and he will be invincible," some one has said. The unconquerable confidence that the Lord has the times and the nations in his hand and that He will fulfill his faithful plans of redemption through judgement, the faith which sees purpose and reason in the course of the world in whatever form this faith has clothed itself, the invincible power in such a faith has come from the prophetic experience of God.[1]

In the prophetic conception of God lies the explanation of the peculiar fact that only the worshippers of Mazda and believers in Jahve have formed a genuinely religious doctrine of the last things. This is due, not to any proximity or contact, which would make possible reciprocal influence. Other peoples have had a longer period of contact with the Persians, but have not absorbed their eschatology. Neither can it be explained as having been brought about by trying conditions or political oppression which served to compress and harden its natural elasticity and vitality for this life into a hope for the future which was to compensate for the sufferings of the present time. Other nations had been threatened and subdued by the Babylonian and Assyrian powers and by other hard taskmasters, in particular had the near blood relatives and neighbours of Israel, Ammon, Moab, Edom, and whatever may be their names, suffered this fate, but have they written apocalypses and proclaimed the judgement of the world?

---

[1] H. Hjärne, *Historiska världsbilder, in Norden,* 1902, pp. 48 f. Reprinted in "Svenskt och Främmande."

IV

History is the true workshop of God. So also is
Nature in its way. "Moses did not withdraw Jahve
from Nature, quite the reverse, Jahve rules over
Nature and reveals himself in it." [1] The religious experience of the prophets, however, rescued the prophetic religion from being caught in *the fatal contradiction of the nature-religions, the contradiction
between Nature and spirit.* For religion inevitably
there comes a time when the naïve confidence in the
deities is shaken and the natural love of life is spent.
Then begins a period of anguish of the soul. The nature deities have no answer for the deeper needs of
salvation. Nature itself and the whole material phenomenal existence is dissolved by the loftier moral attitude and intellectual culture into mere appearance,
a deceptive illusion, as in India, or is made something impure and evil, as in Greece. The longing
for redemption finds no place of rest within the
nature-religions but hurries out beyond the veil into
the great unknown, to the pure and timeless life of

---

[1] C. P. Tiele, *Geschiedenis*, I., 282.

the spirit, the purity of which is conditioned by the radical negation of all that lies within the sphere of earthly existence. The contradiction between the divine and the earthly, between good and evil, blessedness and pain, purity and impurity, is identified with the contrast between the spiritual and the material. This identification reproduces the tragic and heart-rending drama of the perfected nature-religions, as we see it presented in Brahmanism and Buddhism. It is seen also in the Greek redemptive religions even before Plato. Its best known and purest types, however, are Platonism and Neo-Platonism. Both in Plato and Plotinus the thoughts of the beauty of the world and its harmony run parallel. "In Plato dwells the humanist and the mystic as well." The two ideas and interests balance each other and are interwoven one with the other, and have, in their different connections, an interesting and complicated history. But the dualism is never overcome. The inner religious experience, which is fundamental in the nature-religions and culture-religions as well, is such that it knows of no point of rest in the personal, moral and historical life, which would give it a firm foothold and a base of activity in the stream of existence. It flees instead for refuge to the dim,

timeless shore of the stream across which no human
eye can pierce. No light of a life-giving sun shines
over the terrain of existence. The eye cannot pierce
the awesome twilight, which darkens into a star-
less night. Religion still reveals its wonderful powers
in spite of this. But when knowledge of God
and experience of blessedness are weighted down
with the conception of an essential dualism between spirit and body, between rest and activity, and
is sought beyond all positive qualities, the result is,
that the bridge is destroyed between religion on the
one side and all activity for positive ends in the
world, the ethical life and culture, on the other. Culture becomes either a farce or an enemy. Morality
becomes negative. This view, if consistent, must hold
that blessedness requires the stifling of the physical
life or its complete abandonment. Every impulse of
life must be stilled and dulled into insensibility.
"Plotinus, the philosopher of our age,"—Porphyrios
thus begins his biography of the master,—"seems to
feel ashamed that his soul dwells in a body." The
attitude toward life and piety becomes essentially
ascetic. Metaphysical dualism is accompanied by
flight from the world in violent self-torture or else
impassivity, and sets up as the religious ideal the

pure enjoyment of contemplation and ecstasy (as in ecstatic mysticism) or of unbroken tranquillity (as in quietistic mysticism). However high a place morality may reach on the Jacob's ladder which leads to blessedness, it always remains only a means of purification, a way to attain, and never becomes distinctly a service of God.

The prophetic religions of Israel and Iran prove themselves to be the only ones which have broken through this barrier of a contradiction between spirit and body, and have thereby cut the roots of the ascetic ideal of life. This is due to the basic experience of God as redemptive, ethical, loving will. He is too exalted to tolerate any image-making and worship under any outward form. The images of the deities of the advanced Babylonian culture, as well as the images and fetishes of Canaan, were judged by the genuine Mosaism, not as they truly are in the history of polytheism, as an advance together with culture, but as abominations. Neither the images of Jahve as a bull, nor the image of Ahura-Mazda which was worshipped by the great king according to the manner of Mesopotamian art, as shown in the inscription of Darius at Behistun, constitute any real exception to the enmity which the genuine re-

ligions of Moses and Zoroaster always showed
against images of the deity, an enmity which was
astounding to the ancient world and without parallel in the history of religions. Herodotus is sur-
prised that "the Persians do not raise any statues,
temples or altars, but even consider it folly to do so,
for they do not consider, as do the Greeks, that the
gods have any human form." (I, 131.) The development in the prophetic religion, however, is something
entirely different from that which takes place at the
higher stage of nature-religion, when the divine is
conceived of as the abstract unity beyond the multiplicity, as the pure being only negatively to be defined, to make images of which would be absurd
and a return to the naïve stage. Here the standpoint
of culture is something different. The lack of images
in the prophetic religion does not mean that the divine becomes something ethereal and distant, indefinable. Quite the contrary. For the prophetic religion an image means a dead thing (Isaiah 44), but
the Lord is living and active. The image is a created
thing, the Lord is the Creator. The contrast is not
that of spirit versus bodily form, but rather that of
Creator above the created, the living, jealous God
above every image or likeness. The same observa-

tion can be made in reference to the sacrificial cult. In India, long before Buddha, as also in Greece, this was abandoned on the higher stage, as a baser, concrete form, which the spiritual conception did not need, or as a worship which no longer gave comfort to the heart in its longing for redemption. Who does not see that here too the burning, passionate polemic of the prophets in the name of God Himself is of a different order? God does not need sacrifice; He does not want sacrifice, but justice and righteousness.

Does a *monistic* conception belong then to the essence of the prophetic religion? No. In the prophetic religion there emerges another dualism, which is not a metaphysical, speculative one, a contrast between spirit and matter, but a practical, moral and religious dualism. It is not revealed from the beginning. The Daevas against which Zoroaster fought in the name of Ahura-Mazda, were viewed as evil spirits, which was not the case with the Baals, against which Mosaism fought in the name of Jahve. Even the Gathas know a devil, *druj,* "The Lie" *par préférence,* the antagonist, "the evil Spirit," as the name of this power of untruth and death is formulated. He is not a nature deity, nor the material and sensual world, which we know from the Gnostic systems, but the spiritual principle and lord of evil and selfish prudence. The two spirits, between which choice must be made in the battle of life, were found (according to Yasna 30) in the beginning and created first of all, life and death, heaven for the good and hell for the wicked. In the Gathas death only is the territory of "the Evil One." The Lord has created all, light and darkness,[1] sleep and wakefulness, morning, noon and night (Yasna 44). Afterwards all of creation was divided between the two. According to the later view, Anra Mainya created the evil powers, unclean beasts, evil celestial bodies, etc., over against the pure creations of the Lord. But this dualism is never confused with the contrast: spirit versus body. The latter is also named constantly in the *Avesta*. But the devil has his following in the spiritual as well as the physical world. The Lord gave the fravasches, the fylgias, a body with which to fight against evil. His are the pure elements, earth, fire, water. This dualism does not hinder the Mazda religion from being a religion most directly friendly to culture, the most anti-ascetic and optimistic religion that has existed.[2]

---

[1] Cf. Isaiah 45:7.
[2] *Le Génie du Mazdéisme*. Mélanges Ch. de Harlez.

Why did not Zoroaster rather than Buddha become the light of Asia? Why did not the vigorous champion of useful work, of the power of life, purity and health in the rewarding service of the Lord, win the hearts of men, instead of the gentle, sympathetic interpreter of the pain of the world and of Nirvana, the stillness of death? I am not capable of giving the full answer to this complex question, which is bound up with the difference between India and Iran and a series of related historical events. One sentence in the answer must at all events be the following: He had not sufficiently sounded the depths of suffering.[1] The power of a religion is not to be judged by its hymns of praise, but by its experience of the misery and darkness of life. Only *one* religion has gone as far down into the abyss as the religion of the pain of the world, the Indian religion, yes, deeper than the Indian religion. This religion is Christianity. But the message of salvation in the former becomes pessimistic; the true life is the stillness of death. In the latter it becomes optimistic in spite of the infernal depths, an eternal Yea against all Nay, as Carlyle said in briefest form, or in the

---

[1] *La Vie future,* p. 392. Cf. my presentation of the problem of life and death which I have given in this work, chap. V.

apostle's words as these are given in 2 Cor. 1:20: "All the promises of God are yea in Jesus Christ." The revealed religion, perfected in Christianity, is not caught in the metaphysical dualism, but has broken through it by its experience of the will of God through love, acting redemptively in spirit and nature.

For more than a hundred years it has been an axiom that the dualism of later Judaism and of Christianity has come from Parseeism. This is not the place to examine the truth of this opinion. It is sufficient here to say that the dualism in Judaism and Christianity (and Islam) is of the same kind with that in Parseeism, the contrast between God and the devil, between the Divine, victorious will of love and radical, inexplicable evil, between life and death, confidence and despair, heaven and hell, the single combat which we wage in the world between good and evil (Eph. 6:11 ff.). It is not the metaphysical contrast between spirit and matter, unity and multiplicity, indefinable being and the world. Is not the belief in devils recorded in the Gospels as shared by the contemporaries of Jesus, a black spot from the dark times on the bright picture of the joyful message of the gospel? The demand is made, that this dualism can and ought to be removed, as something which has come in from the outside and is essentially foreign and antagonistic. This perhaps is a very common view.[1] I cannot see but that the deeper experience of sin, suffering and distress, which is the strength of religion, by necessity led from the monism of the prophets to the dualism of the Gospels and that this development is one of the most significant within revealed religion. There are not lacking signs of such an insight in modern theology.[2] Jesus has sharpened this dualism, not weakened it. No one has penetrated farther into the problem of evil than he with the words: "An enemy hath done this." Jesus presents no theodicy, no defence for God in the terrible and mysterious trial of sin and misery, defence of the kind which the friends of Job had on their tongues and about which apologetics in all ages has shown much well meaning concern. All attempts within Christianity to escape from or to get over this dualism have either weakened the power which lies in the courageous

---

[1] Cf. W. Bousset, *Die judische Apokalyptik,* 61 f. Bousset adds, however: "The dualism was the covering for the tremendous ethical seriousness and religious depth of the gospel." Thereby the common rationalistic view is overcome.

[2] A. Harnack, *Die Mission und Ausbreitung des Christentums,* 92 ff.

realism of the gospel, or else led to the absurdity of
putting the dualism in the very being of God. This
holds true also of all attempts to make of evil but
a shadow in and for the harmony of the picture, an
element necessary to a higher development. The latter explanation will always have to face the answer
which the Hollander, Robbert Robbertsz, gave two
strict Calvinist ministers, when they sought to put
him in a tight place with the problem of the origin
of sin. "When the first sin was committed Adam put
the blame on the woman and the woman put the
blame on the serpent. The serpent, who was as yet
young and dull, made no answer. Now he has become old and confident and comes to the synod of
Dort and says that God has done it." In Jesus one
seeks vainly for any theory of any sort. The theodicy
of Jesus is not an interpretation for the intellect, but
a task for the will: "Watch and pray." "Deliver us
from evil." It is also a sure confidence of the out-
come: "Now is the judgement of this world, now
shall the prince of this world be cast out." "Every
plant which my heavenly Father planted not, shall
be rooted up." But Jesus also has prevented the dualism of the religious and moral life from becoming
entangled in any dualism of Nature. All of life, all

of existence is its scene. Decision is made in solitude as the soul meets God, who is the God of Jesus Christ and our God. Thence power is received. Afterwards the battle in the moral and cultural life is fought out with positive tasks, with real conquests for the kingdom of God. Luther knows the two kinds of escape from the world. He takes seriously the words of the gospel: "I pray not that thou shouldest take them out of the world, but that thou shouldest keep them from the evil one." It is of this preservation in the midst of life's bitter struggle that Paul sings his song of victory in Romans eighth: "I am persuaded." His words are the echo of those of the psalmist in the 73rd Psalm: "Lord, when I have thee." (Sw. transl.) The battle cry of religion is not: "Gilding the world," nor, "Escape from the world," but, "Overcoming the world."

v

The place of this new experience of God, which in the history of religion constitutes a unique species of revelation, was the soul life of the prophets. They heard the voice of the Eternal and saw his hand outstretched over nations and ages. What was transacted between them and God belongs to the mysteries of the inner life. But in communion with the divine in the invisible sanctuary lies the basis for the clear distinction we can see between prophetic religion and nature-religion, between revealed religion and culture-religion. The investigation of the elemental forms of this higher religious experience belongs to the great and urgent tasks of the psychology of religion. The theological psychology of religion, as exemplified by W. Herrmann has clear insight into the essential difference, but operates with an all too limited material. Its point of view is of great value for the cultivation of religion and for the needs of the church, but leaves out of reckoning important phenomena of essential mysticism within revealed religion, in the Christian era and before Christ as well. The present day psychology of religion in France, in America and England, and other lands as well, has not yet arrived at a decisive recognition of this difference with which we here are concerned. This is due to the fact that in the main it has hitherto concerned itself with more general types and phenomena. In America it has gathered by the statistical method a mass of religious confessions. It has not concentrated its labor upon the great religious personalities, which have handed down to us descriptions of their own inner life. A psychology of religion which does not give its attention primarily to men like St. Paul, Augustine, Luther, Pascal and Kierkegaard, can no doubt make an important and promising contribution. The work of William James is an excellent proof of this. But one cannot expect that it will be able to enter into the deep problems of the psychology of personal mysticism.

May it not be, that this task in scientific religious thought is assigned to Christian thinkers of Scandinavia? It is certain that in the history of our religious thought the significance of the conception and symbol of personality is older and more deeply rooted than elsewhere. In Sweden there has been for at least a century a golden thread running through all of our spiritual culture. This golden thread is that individualistic philosophy, which has as its foremost and typical representative the powerful personality of Erik Gustaf Geijer (Swedish historian, philosopher and poet, 1783–1847). Its matchless architect was the philosopher Boström (Swedish philosopher, called the "Plato of Sweden," 1797–1866). Its refined and profound analyst of the inner life was Pontus Wikner (Swedish philosopher, 1837–1888).

Its universal spirit was Victor Rydberg (Swedish philosopher and poet, 1828–1895). The building erected by Boström was so perfect, so splendid, that for a time it seemed as though the end of all labour had come. Succeeding generations so it seemed, desiring to live and labour must leave the perfected system in its beauty as a glorious mausoleum and seek out other sites if they would build anything new. This did not, however, prove to be the case. Swedish thought, in moving on, has not broken its continuity in the depths. The conception of religion in all genuine preaching in Sweden, in philosophical and theological science, in devotional address, in song and literature testifies to this. In spite of differences on the surface, there is a common appreciation of the significance of personality.

The same is true of Denmark, the land of Kierkegaard and Grundtvig. "However far the thinkers have differed one from another, they have all, as one man, centered upon the principle of personality. It has not, as has continually happened in Germany, been lost sight of, not even by Broechner. At this point, even the Germanized Martensen reveals that he is Danish. This is the height we attained in Kierkegaard. This is where the lasting validity of

Rasmus Nielsen is found. Today every modern thinker in Germany is talking about 'Christian personality.' This language was familiar to us at a time when it was scarcely mentioned in Germany. How has not this idea penetrated all our thinking." [1] The investigation of the psychology of religious experience is foredoomed to be halted before the mystery of the personal individual life. It can, however, serve to bring a clearer light to bear upon an important contrast between two main types of religious experience. I do not here refer to that contrast which exists between an artificial and professional experience, on the one hand, and a genuine and meaningful one on the other. This latter difference is found even in the highest ecstasy of nature mysticism. I refer to that contrast which has already come to our attention. The contrast is between two conceptions of what constitutes communion with God. On the one hand we have the conception that communion with the Divine reaches its culmination in pure ecstatic enjoyment, or in pure indifference as in Nirvana, in which the personal, conscious and volitional life flows out and loses itself as the river in the ocean. On the other

---

[1] E. Lehman, "En tysk Bog og en dansk Betragtning," in *Teologisk Tidskrift* 1903 (IV), 282.

hand we have the conception of communion with God which culminates in the meeting of the prophets with the living God, or in the union of Christ with the Father. The latter conception re-created the personality of the prophets and conveyed new thoughts and new superhuman powers for their task. (Jer. 1.)

The appraisal will be determined by the difference in personal attitudes. Without doubt the prophetic religious experience, with its knowledge of God as a living, active, personal or super-personal almighty power, the Lord of life and history, presents a far more difficult problem for our thought than does the methodical absorption of the soul into the dim and distant depths of being. But no attentive observer can deny the characteristic difference. It is found most clearly in the great personalities, who have been founders of religions. One can compare the prophets of Israel with the great souls, for the most part unnamed, which speak to us in the Upanishads. The supremacy of India in the art of effecting union with the Infinite and in perfecting the theories of this art, was observed already by the ancients. Philostratus puts in the mouth of Appolonius of Tyana the words, "that all wish to live in the nearness of God, but only the Hindus really bring it to pass." Compare for example, Jesus with Buddha! The difference between them according to the comparison made above can thus be expressed: Jesus is a prophet, Buddha a mystic. According to the latter comparison thus: Jesus is the perfect revealer of God, the Son of God, the God-man, Buddha is—the guide to Nirvana! But the two types do not end with these alone. They are continuous also in the many religious personalities of the second, third and fourth order, who confess themselves dependent on the great ones. Because the mysterious, the indivisible and the inexplicable is found in both, we feel constrained to name them both Mysticism, and differentiate between them by calling the one the *mysticism of personality* and the other the mysticism of nature, or perhaps better the *mysticism of infinity*.[1]

The difference lies in the role which the personal life plays. The question is, must the personal life be repressed or extinguished in order to gain the end of religion or attain its higher stages? Or shall it be re-created and purified, so that the natural ego is surrendered and the eternal loving union with God,

---

[1] Cf. *Nutidsbildning och kristlig innerlighet in Förhandlingarna vid studenmötet i Sorö 1903,* reprinted in "När stunderna växla och skrida."

the "image of God" of theology, the "soul spark"
(Funkelein) of the German mysticism of the Middle Ages, is realized and grows into a new man, the
man of God, the concentrated and active life of love
in an ethical personality? Is the way to knowledge
of the Divine the way of negation (*via negationis*),
which leads, as Plotinus says, to the other side of existence, to where the "soul without being good or
evil or anything," without consciousness of body or
spirit, receives the divine? Must we, with Hiero-
theus, reach "the mysterious, silent stillness, which
dissolves consciousness and form," or again with the
Areopagite, or Eckhart, or Ruysbroek arrive at "the
divine darkness," "the nameless, formless nothing." [1]
Or, is the way to God a way of affirmation (*via posi-
tionis*), which leads through a complete self-renunci-
ation and self-denial to a richer and stronger personal life; to the revelation of the divine will of love
in the most glowing, most perfect and most nobly
formed personal life, that of Jesus Christ? This way
reveals its presence by many good and wonderful
gifts, but nowhere is it nearer God nor does it ever
know a higher attitude toward God and a richer
fulness of God than in the highest endowment of

---

[1] W. R. Inge, *Christian Mysticism,* 97, 103, 182.

life: personal love built on the foundation of a living trust in God. This love is a warm, human reality, whether in suffering or in jubilant joy. It is entirely different from the self-sacrifice of mysticism, which is at bottom a cold thing, although it is capable of complete renunciation without complaint or even of suffering martyrdom in flames at the stake (1 Cor. 12, 13). Is God the great, silent sea of infinity, which yearns to have the individual broken fragments float together again, formless and nameless, to slumber in its mysterious embrace? Or is God the overmastering, enkindling and burning holy love, which wills and generates personal life? Is He not interpreted to us only in a personal life of love, so that the word will be true which says, 'Outside this human being God is not to be found (*Extra hunc hominem nullus Deus reperitus*)?' Are we not nearest him and most like him when we rejoice in our personal life and in the attainment of the deepest self by losing the selfish ego?

The vindication of personality in this sense is the very opposite of a self-glorifying demand for the rights of the individual. Harald Hjärne, the Swedish historian, in an essay on Lafcadio Hearn, the Amer-

ican revealer of Japan, points out the complete mis-
conception which this Greek-Irish-North American
has of the solidarity of Japanese society. Lafcadio
Hearn in his antipathy against the noisy individualism and dogmatic lordship of the Western world,
has confused this solidarity which is founded on religion, with what Hjärne calls 'the cloud-kingdom
of impersonal mysticism.' Hjärne writes: "He is mistaken—we can safely say so on the basis of his own
testimony. What he has seen is not the destruction
of personality, but its resurrection into a richer life
in an unbroken continuity with a rejuvenated society. From the depths of magic there emerge only
powers of darkness, which bind the conscious and
responsible life of the spirit. Any will-power which
is directed to higher things is never a drive toward
extinction of the personal life. It is the very core of
personality, which is strengthened more and more
in the degree in which the call to higher things is
heard and becomes more clear. Every social community is built upon the foundation of a personal,
self-sacrificing will. If the foundation is undermined
the building will fall. The height to which the structure can rise is conditioned in the sustaining strength

of the foundation. All history, that of the ancient world and of our own forefathers, bears testimony to this fact."

Two points of contrast between revealed religion and the religion of mysticism are connected with this difference which we have above indicated. First, as to personal authority. The religious relation of one person to another in the mysticism of infinity, becomes at best something impersonal, a prescription, an indication, an illumination, knowledge of the way to attain experience. The influence and authority of great personalities play a very important role in the mysticism of infinity, it is true, for such are the necessary conditions in human life. But this influence of personalities is really fundamentally antagonistic to the essence of a mysticism, which transcends time and history. Within the trinity of Buddhism *dhamma,* doctrine indication or direction, is without doubt the most important element.[1] The heroes of the highest religious development of the Greeks, Socrates, Plato and Plotinus reject all claim to be authorities. They do this in the interest of purity in the relation to God. Christian mysticism also

---

[1] Cf. my book, *Treenighest,* p. 16 ff.

has felt that a personal, religious relation to Jesus Christ, as shown in the Gospels and in history, was a burden and an imperfection. "Mysticism is a specific form of religion, namely a piety which feels that the historical in the positive religions is a burden from which it would free itself." (W. Herrmann). "The Bible is a safeguard against all mysticism which is alien toward history. Mysticism would know only of the innermost immediacy in relation to God. Feeling and imagination alone are valid as organs of the religious life. Society and history are viewed as hindrances to the religious life and must, so much as possible, be rejected in favor of the inner life." (M. Kähler.) In the Bible itself the problem of these differences comes to light. The attempt is made to solve it by the short-cut of mystical religion. But the problem which is made actual by the critical investigation of the Scriptures proves to be too complex for such an easy solution. Mysticism eludes the ancient and fundamental Christian question: How can we reconcile the fact that Christianity is indissolubly joined to a phenomenon in time, namely the indispensable authority of Jesus, with the claim that Christianity is the absolute religion, exalting the religious relation above all risks of relativity?[1]

Within the revealed religion personal authority is an integral part of religion and is recognized as such. This is true already of the Old Testament prophets. Revelation is bound up with their personalities. Wellhausen has with his keen insight seen this. He says: "It belongs to the prophetic, the genuine idea of revelation, that Jahve, above the beyond all ordered mediation, communicates himself to the individual, the chosen one, in whom the mysterious, indivisible relation in which the Deity stands to human beings is exalted and becomes active. Apart from the prophets, that is, in abstracto, there can be no revelation. Revelation exists for and in the human ego. Hereby arises the synthesis of seeming contradictions. The subjective in its highest significance, exalted above all rules, is the truly objective, the divine."

This connection between religion and the chosen men of God was not broken in the progress of development, so that it cannot be considered a lower, pedagogical measure. Rather, in the history of religion,

---

[1] The problem has been set in all its bearings in the important work of E. Troeltsch, *Die Absolutheit des Christentums und die Religionsgeschichte.*

the unheard of has happened, which has created
the paradox of Christianity. Revealed religion has
reached its perfection, not in a perfect doctrine or
guide to salvation, but in a person. "For other foundation can no man lay than that which is laid, which
is Jesus Christ." In this person the Divine and human, the objective and the subjective are fused. He
stands at the same time "as the perfection of divine
love and of human faithfulness," (Frederick Fehr),
and mediates the communion of his own with God.
The principle of personality is the strength of Evangelical Christianity. It knows only one authority, the
authority of personality.[1]

In the second place, mystical religion in the abstract sense is attainable only for the upper ten thousand of spiritual culture and refinement. They only
have the time and the ability to procure for themselves the experience in question. Mystic religions
are essentially aristocratic and must be decked out
in an exoteric garment if they are to be accessible to
those "who labour and are heavy laden."

Jesus praises his heavenly Father because He has

---

[1] Cf. Harald Höffding, *Religionsfilosofi*, 241 ff., 275 ff. If the lines of
thought, which he presents, are drawn out to their conclusions, which
they are not, they lead to the authority of the evangelical religion, the
personal authority of Jesus.

hidden this from the wise and revealed it unto babes. To have a vision of God requires a pure heart and a clear and true personality, not knowledge, not an art or a method. To know him there is needed the heart of a child, not philosophy. The prophets and Jesus addressed themselves to the conscience, to the elementary ethical censor in man. They depend upon its sanction. The sign which Jesus gave was the sign of Jonah, the sign of the prophet, of the preaching of repentance. Technicalization is the worst hindrance of the Gospel. Jesus cannot tolerate Pharisees, but he goes in to eat with sinners and publicans. The authority of his apostles was not based on extraordinary experiences, although they possessed such. They offered their credentials thus:—"by the manifestation of the truth, commending ourselves to every man's conscience in the sight of God."

Two misconceptions must here be removed. Ethical elements are not lacking in the mysticism of nature and the mysticism of infinity. On the contrary, the ethical is given a more and more prominent place in the process of "Purification," in those means by which communion with God is brought about. This is true beyond as well as within Christianity, in India, in Platonism, Neo-Platonism, Sufism and the

mysticism of the Middle Ages.[1] But here the actual
communion with God is affected "beyond good and
evil." (*Jenseits von Gut und Böse.*) It is not that the
personal life in its fulness of ethical character and
vital energy is filled and strengthened. It is repressed
in this communion with God. In the religion of the
monks, which is a mysticism of infinity, personality
entirely disappears. It is not simply chance, that in
the first order of monks which Pachomius gathered,
the brethren were designated and classified by the
letters of the alphabet.[2] Ethics becomes an ascetic
practice, a self-discipline for the purpose of tran-
scending every "creaturely" thing, not a direct service of God with a positive end, the Kingdom of God.
The Reformers could make the accusation against
their opponents, that they were not able to say how
the Holy Spirit is given and how good works are
produced. William James is right when he points
out that no one and nothing in Roman Catholic theology can speak with such a heart for sick souls as
does Martin Luther.

And further, the difference between the mysticism
of personality and the mysticism of infinity does not

---

[1] Cf. W. R. Inge, *Christian Mysticism.*
[2] See L. Moltesen, *Det Kristne Munkvoesen,* p. 104.

imply that unusual, abnormal physical and psychical phenomena, such as visions, ecstatic conditions, are banished from the former. God can permit his power and love to be revealed in heavenly visions and notable raptures. Decisive experiences in revealed religion can be clothed in such forms. The disciples on the Mount of Transfiguration and Paul on the road to Damascus are proofs of this. Many of the prophets had clairvoyant and passionate experiences of soul, such as characterized the Canaanitish *"nabies."* Others had none.[1] Such experiences are not restricted to the period of revelation, but appear in our day in the experiences of many Christians, in proportion to their personal endowments and the ways of God. S. Michelet calls attention to the revelation given Hans Nielsen Hauge, April 5, 1796. Many other examples can be given. But the difference between these and the experiences of the other forms of mystical religion is clear.

1. In the revealed religion the extraordinary states of soul are lacking entirely in some of the greatest personalities. I am not now exclusively concerned

---

[1] S. Michelet, *Israels profeter som åbenbaringens boerere,* in "Religionsvetenskapliga kongressens i Stockholm förhandlingar," 1897, p. 494 ff. Muhammed was a visionary, but was anxious not to be classed with the professional ecstatics of his day.

with the fact that there is related of Jesus no ecstatic feature, still less ecstasy in a technical sense, for Jesus has a place all his own. The greatest of the prophets, Jeremiah, lacks every trace of ecstasy. Neither did Luther have any ecstatic experiences.

2. Where they are found, they are never adduced as a necessary condition of attaining communion with God, nor are they claimed to be the highest or the essential thing in religion. St. Paul is forced to overcome his modesty when he tells of his visions and revelations in the second letter to the Corinthians. In 1 Cor. 12:31 and ch. 13 he makes up the table of precedence and puts love above such extraordinary manifestations as that of speaking with tongues.

Ecstatic experiences occur in all nature-religions as the highest and essential communion with God. At lower stages this is manifested in violent forms, at higher stages in purer and nobler forms. For practical purposes, for guidance in religion, the most ancient form of a psychology of religion comes to light even in the nature-religions. In India and Greece the conditions and stages of the ecstatic experience were studied and described with extraordinary penetration and refinement. Those who noted them have become the teachers both of the Eastern and of the

Western World, in the East in Sufism, in the West in Christian mysticism. Historical and literary influence is evident. But because of the fact that human nature is everywhere the same, the Jacob's ladder of ecstasy everywhere becomes essentially the same, even though no influence of one religion upon another has taken place.[1] In its most refined form ecstasy, in a technical sense, is a most exalted and refined enjoyment of the infinite. It is vastly different from the sensual, emotional intoxication of the lower forms of mysticism. It tends on analysis to evaporate. Ecstasy, in a technical sense, is an experience outside of consciousness. It nowise corresponds to that which in common parlance is summed up under the term "ecstatic experience." It is not the same as St. Paul's experience which he describes in 2 Cor. 12, for he remembered what he had heard and seen.

3. Ecstasy in the proper sense of the word, which is the goal of the mysticism of infinity, is unthinkable as a form for the higher experience of revealed religion. For revealed religion includes knowledge

---

[1] The mysticism of infinity is everywhere similar. Maeterlinck in *Le Trésor des Humbles* finds that Ruysbroek "although he did not know it was influenced by Platonism in Greece, Sufism in Persia, Brahmanism in India and Buddhism in Thibet." W. R. Inge, *Christian Mysticism,* 171 f.

of the living God and a revelation of his nature. Ecstasy on the other hand, shuts out all positive knowledge and every communication of truth. We must not, in the interest of rationality, set aside and disregard the extraordinary mental states through which God communicates with man according to his good pleasure. Proofs in favor of extraordinary experiences and the mystery of religion [1] are heartily welcome to counteract the weight which we lay upon the satisfaction of the mind. Still, it would be a poor corrective to fall into nature mysticism. Whatever of holy memories God may wish to afford, in quiet or in great raptures, in voices, in visions, which will shine through and illuminate the whole of life, this is his good pleasure. We must not, however, build the religious life on the basis of that which cannot and must not be mentally grasped. We must not exchange the valuation which St. Paul has given us for that of the mysticism of infinity.

Within that complex religious creation which is called Christianity, not only the prophetic religion but also the Aryan nature-religion and culture-religion were continued, although its mysticism of infinity received a strong Christian modification. In part this

---

[1] B. Duhm, *Das Geheimniss in der Religion.*

consisted in the consciousness of the living God, which was an active inheritance from the Gospel, while consistency with the point of view of the past tended toward pantheism and abstract idealism. In part it consisted in visionary elements taken from a conception of Christ which was more or less detached from history. And finally it consisted partly in Christian ethics. Within Christianity as it developed, the two chief types of the cultivation of the inner life can be studied. There is a mixed form with a manifold of nuances which we find in such mystics as the Areopagite, Bernard, Meister Eckhart, Theresa, Wordsworth, and Amiel. Then there are such personal mystics as Augustine, who returned finally to the Christian impressions of his childhood, Luther, Pascal, John Bunyan, Vinet, Kierkegaard, Wikner (a Swedish philosopher). Luther himself had been fascinated by the mystic religion, the genuine, noble flower of the Middle Ages, which lived its life of imperishable beauty in the very midst of doctrines of works, sacramental magic, worldly ambitions for power and the weeds of decadence. We remember the warm recommendation which Luther gave the *German Theology,* which he published in its entirety in 1518. Later on, Luther had to meet a different manifestation of mysticism in Carlstadt and the prophets of Zwickau, who held an unevangelical doctrine of a contradiction between soul and body, between the inner and the outer life, and had gone over to the side of legalism. When Luther, in opposition to these, developed his own doctrine of liberty through Christ in faith and love,[1] in his zeal, he made no distinction between the *Schwärmer* and the mystics who were true to the best traditions of mysticism. In this he was unjust.

It is clear that Luther, with the exclusiveness, the prepossession, which sometimes characterizes religious genius, was not then able to see that the mystic religion was another basic type with legitimate claims in its species, possessed of beauty and truth and feeling. He could not see that it was at home in the world of inner warmth and devotion to God.

Luther has with incomparable richness and clarity described "the communion of the Christian with God" according to the character of revealed religion, as contrasted with the sublime mysticism of infinity. Faith and confidence are expressions of personal relations. Through basing his faith on Christ, on the

---

[1] "Glaube und liebe," is the constantly recurring theme in the tract, "Wieder die himmlischen Propheten."

revelation of God, and not on any ambiguous or uncertain experiences of his own in the form of a mystical emotional life or of a fulfilling of the law, Luther won his certainty of salvation. In this assurance of salvation and in the doctrine of the intimate connection of the new life with faith, Luther has indicated the distinguishing mark of personal religion, for the humblest Christian man as well as for great and chosen souls. In a clear and simple way he has shown the victory over mysticism and, as well, over legal religion.[1] He says of his opponents: "They nowhere teach how we can be rid of sin, receive a good conscience and win a peaceful and happy heart before God, which is the most important of all."

As against the "enthusiasts," the *Schwärmer*, Luther has also pointed out a psychological mark of identification of the religious experience which belongs to the mysticism of personality. This is the *terrores conscientiae*, the terror of conscience (*Frygt og Baeven* of Kierkegaard), a phrase which, with precision, defines the difference between his religion and the mysticism of infinity and marks the

---

[1] See the discussion of the subject by A. Harnack in *Dogmenge-schichte*.

personal, ethical character of the former and its consciousness of the power of God. I quote Luther's
letter to Melanchton, January 13, 1522. He urges
Melanchton to test the alleged prophets. He was to
question them to ascertain "if they have any experience of spiritual tribulations and the divine birth
pangs, death and hell. If you hear only of pleasant
delights, of tranquillity, devotion (as they will call
it) and piety, you must discredit them, even if they
claim to have been exalted to the third heaven." Because of the weight I attach to the following text, I
quote it in the original.

"*Quaeras, num experti sint spirituales illas angustias
et nativitates divinas, mortes, infernosque. Si audieris
blanda, tranquilla, devota (ut vocant) et religiosa, etiamsi
in tertium coelum sese raptos dicant, non approbabis.*
Quia signum filii hominis deest, qui est βάσανος, probator
unicus Christianorum et certus spirituum descretor. Vis
scire locum, tempus, modum colloquiorum divinorum?
audi: *sicut leo contrivit omnia ossa, et projectus sum a
facie oculorum tuorum, et repleta est malis anima mea,
et vita mea inferno appropinquavit.* Non sic loquitor
Majestas (ut vocant) immediate, ut homo videat, imo,
non videbit me homo, et vivet. Et stellam parvam ser-
monis ejus non fert natura. Ideo enim per homines loqui-
tur, quod loquentum ipsum ferre omnes non possumus.

Nam et virginem turbavit angelus, sic et Danielem, *sic et Jermias queritur: corripe me in judicio, et non sis tu mihi formidini.* Et quid plura? Quasi Majestas possit cum vetere homine loqui familiariter, et non prius occidere atque exsiccare, ne foeteant odores ejus pessimi, cum sit ignis consumens. Etiam somnia et visiones sanctorum sunt terribiles saltem, postquam intelliguntur. Tenta ergo et ne Iesum quidem audias glorisum, nisi videris prius crucifixum." [1]

It is true that this word about terror of conscience, *terrores conscientiae,* which Melanchton, not from his own experience but from Luther's, has made a part of the *Apology for the Augsburg Confession* of 1531 and set up as the necessary condition for cer-

---

[1] 'For the sign of the Son of Man is lacking, which is the touchstone, the only mark of a Christian and the sure divider of the spirits. Would you know the place, the time and the manner of conversation with God, listen: "The lion crushes all their bones (Dan. 6:24)"; "My soul is full of troubles and my life draweth near to Sheol (Ps. 88:3)." The Divine Majesty does not speak, as they say, immediately, so that a man may see it. Nay, "no man can see me and live (Ex. 33:20)." Human nature cannot endure even a little of the speech of God. He speaks through men, for we could not endure the speaker himself. Even the Virgin was terrified by the angel. So also Daniel. And Jeremiah cries: "Correct me, O Lord, but in moderation (Jer. 10:24)." "Be not a terror unto me (17:17)." And what more? As though the Divine Majesty could speak intimately with the "old man" and not first kill it or dry it up, so that its worst smells may not stink when the fire consumes it. Even the dreams and visions of the saints are terrifying, when they are understood. Examine and you will find that not even Jesus was exalted before he was crucified.'

tainty of faith, has caused confusion and led to a
certain unnaturalness in Lutheran piety. One must
concede that Spener is right when he says that experience differs among Christians. "With some the
process is more lenient. The power of the law is
hardly felt before the comfort of the Gospel heals
all." [1] It is wrong and unpsychological to make the
experience of the great hero of faith the standard for
all. The penalty has been paid in the mechanization
of repentance and a lapse into emotional and legal
religion.

On the other hand it will not do to explain, as do
Ritschl and Harnack, the *terrores conscientiae* of
Luther, his "spiritual tribulations" (*angustias spirituales*), his experience of "death and hell" (*mortes et
infernos*), as being caused by his individual situation and the ignorance of salvation in which his
church had held him. Such experiences are not peculiar to Luther. They are found also in men of God
of revealed religion in the Holy Scriptures, on whom
Luther builds in the letter quoted. They have been
verified by many, known and unknown, since his
day. Even today they are often marks of a deep and
vital religious experience. They are not necessarily

---

[1] A. Ritschl, *Geschichte des Pietismus*, II, 113.

the result of reflection on the sense of guilt, but they are the reaction of the whole human personality to the infinite holiness and majesty of God.

Luther does not exclude extraordinary and ecstatic experiences of those who have real communion with the living God. He speaks implicitly of "the dreams and visions of the saints." They are neither made necessary conditions nor are they excluded. Herein is revealed the spiritual and ethical character of the mysticism of personality. In the mysticism of infinity the highest and essential communion with God is bound up with a carefully specified physical and psychic preparation, namely ecstasy. A refined and ethereal, but not invisible, remnant from the primitive nature-religion, is thus revealed in the ennobled religious self-discipline of culture-religion.

The words of Luther to Melanchton, who was less at home in the depths of spiritual experience, give us a firm grasp on the psychological distinction between the two types of religious experience. The identifying marks of the mysticism of infinity are "pleasant delights, tranquillity, devotion, piety" (*blanda, tranquilla, devota et religiosa*). St. Francis heard the angel drawing the bow across the strings of the celestial violin. The infinite sweetness and

beauty of the tone was such, that one more stroke
would have brought him death in complete blessedness. The mysticism of infinity in its pure form,
seeks its way out to the point of union with the
divine by leaving, by degrees, the creaturely, divest-
ing itself of all qualities, pushing slowly out beyond
the sole distinction of existence and non-existence,
being and non-being. Beyond the last cliffs of conscious life lies the goal, wrapped in mist. It is without space and form, without name and outline that
can be remembered. The moments spent in genuine
ecstasy cannot even be described, for consciousness
is extinguished. They are surrounded by an inexpress-
ible sanctity and given an ethereal fragrance. During the time that Porphyrios abode with his admired
master, Plotinus four times experienced union with
that divine life which is in all that exists.[1] The
purest element of ecstasy consists in a liberty, won
step by step, until the outermost limits of life are
reached.

How different is the world of personal mysticism!
Jeremiah, St. Paul, Augustine, Luther, Pascal,
Kierkegaard, cry out: "Lord, spare me! Depart from
me! My guilt!" (*O, culpa mea!*) The miserable

----

[1] *Vita Plotini*, XXIII.

human creature quakes and shivers, bleeds and moans. In mysticism of infinity we see an outstretched hand, a longing, dreaming gaze. In the mysticism of personality we see a man, who shrinks back in dread and dares not even lift up his eyes. In the former there is an ascension, in the latter a struggle in the darkness of death. Under the mighty grasp of God the recipient of God's grace shudders. He cannot escape and he would not escape. He kisses and blesses the hand of God, for it lifts him up into another world, into the blessed kingdom of life and so holds him secure, so safe, that he can defy sin and death and the Devil. In the former we have liberty in the dim spaces of infinity; in the latter, liberty in the mighty hand of God. In the former a struggle toward the One, the great and unutterable One; in the latter, a meeting in quiet places perhaps, but also in the desert, in labour, with an attacking, living, active Will; with an overflowing, empowering fulness of personal life of holiness and love, in comparison with which all else that is called life is but a disappointment, an illusion. In the one, the great stillness, the distant unfathomable depths of Divinity; in the other, a living God, unutterably active, who crushes us, but also saves us.

I shall not carry further this comparison between the ecstatic enjoyment and the *"terrores"* and *"angustiae"* of personal mysticism. As we study the peculiar and distinctive forms of communion with God both within and outside revealed religion, we cannot escape the strong impression that, in the mysticism of personality, God conducts himself, if I may speak thus naïvely and in human ways about the activity of the unfathomable God, in a manner entirely different from that observed in the other. He is active, intervening, self-communicating, attacking, revealing, standing forth in the life of the soul as in the world of history.[1] All this is on the supposition that we feel obliged to make the metaphysical venture of faith from the subjective experiences of the human soul to God and his work. If we proceed from experience to the Experienced One, we find that a part of the field of the inner life detaches itself and is marked as the area of a *special revelation of God.*

Ecstasy in its specific sense does not characterize the important and essential experiences of personal mysticism. Tribulations (*"angustiae"*) and terrors (*"terrores"*) are foreign to genuine mysticism of in-

---

[1] Cf. E. G. Geijer, *Föreläsningar över människans historia,* 217.

finity. Yet, we are mindful of the fact that there is one, and only one, who possesses and transmits at the burning centre of his personal life of love the infinite fulness of God's being. This one is Jesus Christ. In the unsearchable purity of his communion with the Father he does not show a sign of ecstasy, but neither does he show *"terrores"* and *"angustiae,"* such as men of God before and since his time have felt. Gethsemane and Golgotha are places of anguish beyond all anguish, distress beyond all distresses. But never do we hear from his lips, "O my guilt!"

The Christian Church cannot build its certainty of possessing the revelation of God, the word of God through prophets and through Christ, on the results of historical and psychological investigation. The Church cannot wait in uncertainty until this investigation is completed. She builds her assurance on her own experience and testimony, verified by every regenerate soul. The same is true for dogmatic theology, which is the scientific interpretation of the self-consciousness of the Church.[1] It is, however, of supreme importance that the claims which underlie such a certainty be investigated in the light of the

---

[1] Cf. L. Ihmels, *Die Selbständlichkeit der Dogmatik gegenüber der Religionsphilosophie.*

entire historical reality of religion on our earth. It is then revealed in a surprising way that the certainty of revelation which the Church possesses is not reduced to that kind of certainty which every other religion claims for its object. Instead it is found that there is a very deep and marked difference within the world of religion itself as it is revealed in history and in the inner life of the soul. The science of religion has not as yet got its eye fixed on this specific line of demarcation in the history of religion. It is still so dazzled by its own variegated and rich field of labour, so full of joy at having attained its liberty from the bondage of ecclesiastical formulations—a liberty which has brought welfare and comfort not to itself alone, but to the Church as well—that it has not discovered this boundary line. Ultimately the fact of this difference will gain attention and make possible a far more detailed investigation than these pages afford.

This distinction, however, must not be pressed too far. Our human understanding is so constituted that for purposes of study we must separate that which in reality is interwoven. Let us sum up our findings. The history of religion reveals to us two types of communion with God. In the one, the subject considers the goal of religion to be reached in the loss of self. I and Thou are to become identical. The climax in this mysticism is reached in the soul of man becoming identified with deity. *"Tat tvam asi." "I am God."* The other form attains communion with God by losing the self, the limited, selfish ego, but not by extinction, submergence in the sea of infinity, but through realizing its true nature in God. There is in this communion no cessation of communicated interchange between an I and the Thou. The soul is mastered by the majesty of God, by his power and grace, so that it is no longer able to speak or distinguish clearly. The depth of spiritual communion finds at last no words, no adequate expression for its reality. Here also is an ecstasy, an exaltation above the conscious. But the unity with the divine is one of fellowship of the human and the divine, not of absorption and extinction of the human in the divine.

We find these two types of religion in some instances in a pure form. But in most cases we can trace something of the one and of the other in the same individual. The fundamental difference comes to light, when either discipline and absorption becomes the chief end, or else the revelation and intervention of God.

II

THE PORTALS OF REVELATION

The Organs of Religion in Man

WHEN we speak of revelation[1] in this connection, it cannot mean anything less than
knowledge of the essential nature of reality. It must
be added, however, that it means also an insight, a
penetration, which satisfies not only a more or less
powerful intellectual faculty in us, but one which
gives to our very being that point of contact which
it needs for its vital power, for salvation and for the
realization of our true dignity.

Revelation means still more. The word has something to say about the manner in which this knowledge is imparted. Revelation implies that man is
the one who receives, God the one who communicates himself. Seers and wise men, and ordinary religious persons as well, have in all ages and in
widely separated religions borne testimony to the
experience of the self-communication of the divine,
to the certainty of truth, of God, of the spirit, of

---

[1] Cf. *Religionsproblemet II*, by the author.

salvation. They have also testified that this comes as a gift. There must be a search, it is true, but revelation is not something which can be seized as booty but is received without price. Obviously we have here to do with a psychological fact, verified also outside the area of religion, within that of creative art. Insight comes instantaneously. Certainty spreads through the mind like a light from heaven. The truth shines forth like lightning. But when we here speak of revelation, we are not satisfied with merely recognizing such a way of working of the human soul. If such a breaking forth of clarity and certainty is nothing more than a particular form of the psychic process, we cannot know whether or not we have to do with a deeper reality. The word revelation would then be used, not in a real sense and would not necessarily correspond to reality.

Here we are met by the great problem, always in the centre of the battle, either denied or affirmed: "Can we have any knowledge of super-sensual reality in or behind that which our senses perceive? Are we helplessly shut out from a real revelation because of the very nature of our means of knowledge? Or is it possible for us to possess communication with the spiritual world?"

In regard to this problem, which has been and is being answered in different ways by philosophy, I shall point out two actual facts. The variation of views in this matter stands in close relation to the drift of the age and its ruling methods of work. The tendency to deny the possibility of revelation may be due to a certain fatigue of the intellect after an epoch of great daring in metaphysical thought. Or else it may arise out of the fact that the demands of our civilization direct the attention and labour so energetically and exclusively to that which is nearest at hand, to the investigation and practical application of our material resources, the facts of history and the investigation of the human mind, that there is no strength left for metaphysics, for the questions concerning the real meaning of our existence, which are capable of so many interpretations. For a considerable time, yet not for all time, can this attitude of concern only for that which the eye can see, convey so strong an impression of the massive solidity of material things, that the spiritual reality seems like a world of mist and dreams. It cannot be for long. Only give the human intellect time enough and science will itself dissolve this seemingly compact and solid reality into symbols and signs upon which the human spirit can never find rest and build a real insight into truth, a faith and a conviction.

The generations immediately preceding ours and we ourselves have lived through a period in which metaphysical problems have been thrust aside, both because of fatigue after the heat of an age of creative effort, and also because of an intensive concentration on the empirical and technical perhaps unique in the history of civilization. We are now experiencing along the whole line a double phenomenon. On the one hand we are not satisfied with merely using the methods of natural science to benefit mankind by inventions and by the art and technique of medicine and surgery. We are examining the worth and the meaning of knowledge itself. And this is being done not only by professional philosophers and critics in the field of the knowledge process. Even those who pursue the exact and the descriptive sciences turn about and examine their own methods asking: What can these methods, these experiments and theories really give us, and what are they unable to give? From all this has come the insight, that the basic theories of natural science have meaning and value only in the degree in which they are conceived as tools for the control of nature, but that they become contradictory if one expects through them to arrive at knowledge of what reality truly is. No one can halt at the mere insight and hypotheses of natural science in certainty, silent or expressed, that we have found in the atoms or in the ether the mystery of reality. The critical examination of science itself has driven the scientists of our day out of such a position.

But not only this. At the same time there has come a great wave of interest in the problem of reality itself. Where are we and whither are we moving? Can we be certain of anything? If we can, what is the nature of that reality upon which our thought and faith can obtain a foot-hold? I am not thinking now of the bizarre and curious oddities, in which, not seldom, metaphysics has taken refuge when thrust to one side. I am thinking of the newly awakened metaphysical interest and a fresh confidence which characterizes the critical thinking of our day. We cannot and we will not be satisfied agnostically to renounce any positive certainty, just as little as we can any longer be rocked to sleep in an uncritical dogmatism of metaphysics. The tendency of the thought of the age is to enquire as to the possibility, yes, to feel the vital necessity of insight into the nature of reality itself. But we have lost much of our confidence in the methods of knowledge with which both rational idealism and materialism have worked.

Before I proceed to the three fundamental phenomena in human personality in which revelation has chiefly been sought or recognized and from which, according to my conviction, it issues, there is needed a word about the approximative or symbolic character of our understanding of what revelation is. I am not here pleading for scepticism. On the contrary, I shall maintain in what follows, that an assured certainty can be reached, which together with a clearly defined form belongs to the very essence of revelation. But we must give over the habit of reasoning about the mystery of reality and of God, as though it were like the question of an equation, or of the politics of the Kaiser, or, of the canals of Mars. How insipid and pretentious some ways of treating the greatest of all problems must appear to any one who has had a vital appreciation of the rich and mysterious, the imposing and unfathomable complexity into which we enter as but infinitesimal elements. Examples of clear and firm attitudes toward life, of unswerving convictions, such that a man could die for them, assuredly do not involve also the ability adequately to express them. How have not prophets and apostles felt that! We, creeping creatures of earth, seek to grasp in comprehensive symbols the decisive experiences which history and life give us. Human would-be-wisdom easily conceals under a prudent logical precision the lack of genuine, vital experience. Instead of that urgent and intimate contact with reality which alone brings salvation with insight into truth, there is substituted a sort of juggling with terms and symbols, which in its self-confidence loses the thing itself, exchanging it for an empty form. The feeling of the wonderful and inconceivable riches which lie behind all our terms for the divine should keep alive our consciousness of the provisional, the incomplete character of these terms. The usefulness and transparency of the symbols does not mean that they are perfectly grasped rationally. It means that we ought never—I say never—to use them,—God, reality, truth, heavenly Father, the personality of God, being, life,—unless the miracle of reality shimmers through them. If dust and grime are permitted to collect on these windows—for that is what these re-

ligious terms of ours are—or, if we actually paint
them over to keep the light from blinding us, we
no longer will discern anything of that spiritual
world which they would reveal to us. Instead we see
only them, the signs instead of the things signified,
the windows instead of the light and the figure they
are meant to transmit. Beyond question we have
lost out of much of our spiritual language, old and
new, learned and unlearned, that background of
reality which alone transforms the words from
empty sounds, which really means that we profane
and blaspheme the holy things, into participation in
reality and life.

Even when we stand before a human being we
can perceive how utterly impossible it is for us to
express the reality of his being or to put it into a
comprehensive formula or term. How much more
difficult must it be to fix in words, which of course,
only can be symbols—because the thing is beyond
the senses—the conviction of the basic power of
reality, or God. This does not by any means imply
that we can be careless or uncertain as to the terms
we use for reality, as if it could be represented to us
in almost any way you please, or as if you may exchange one symbol for another, as for example im-

personality for personality in the being of God, or dualism for monism in our own religious views. No indeed, an absolute certainty can easily be combined with a vital feeling that it is incomprehensible. Such we find that St. Paul possessed in relation to the being and ways of God.

The portals for revelation in the human personality are three, the intellect or understanding, the intuition of infinity, with its emphasis on feeling, and the urge of the ideal, or the conscience. The three are by no means of equal value.

I

We have already spoken of the very restricted use of the intellect as a source of knowledge of reality. Modern critical science harks back in different ways to Kant. But he was by no means the first to show the limited sphere of the intellect. The great thinkers and religious men of all times, Plato and Plotinus, St. Paul and St. Augustine, Luther and Pascal, and Hindu thinkers as well, have given expression to the experience, that insight into the being of reality does not come through the analysing investigation and logical conclusions of the understanding, but rather through intuition, through surrender to authority, through will and faith. Culture reveals that if the intellect is allowed to exert a one-sided rule to the exclusion of other powers in human life the result is a dissolution of certainty and also of initiative. Reality is dissolved into misty vagueness. If the intellect is depended upon as a source of truth, as being able to satisfy the thirst for pure truth and to reveal the essence of reality, it will be found, on the one hand to be impotent by reason of its abstractness, or on the other hand to be liable to lead us astray and to dissolve all certainty. If we conceive it, however, as a means to practical ends, if we look upon it as a servant of life rather than as a master— a master who becomes an unmerciful tyrant—the intellect possesses marvellous power and has a task of its own. Its task is not to penetrate into the meaning of reality, but to labour for the good of humanity by means of its working hypotheses. By means of these hypotheses it brings to the surface and makes available for the technician the materials which can be used for the welfare of the human organism and for the purpose of civilization. From this it is not to be inferred that the intellect plays only an insignificant part in the sphere of revelation. This error has cost humanity an appalling price. In religion it is poor policy to be miserly and suspicious toward the claims of the intelligence and weak and compliant toward self-satisfied obscurantism. There are many persons for whom religion is chiefly a matter of worldly concern, providing a platform for agitation or a field for self-seeking ambitions. It is no wonder that such persons seem unable to understand an interest in religion which is not bound up with worldly purposes. For such minds there is no such thing as an unmixed striving to attain knowledge of the truth in religion. There are, however, others for whom religion means salvation and is a concern of the inner life above all else. These ought never to forget that unwarranted claims of the intellect in religion cannot be answered by mere protests. The only effective answer is the discovery of the real sources and conditions of revelation in the life of the human spirit. This is gained only by an intense spiritual labour.

The task of the intellect in revelation is as important as it is extensive. First and last it constitutes an indispensable control. Without its weeding and trimming the plants of religion will grow wild. The criticism of the understanding is essential. Else zeal will degenerate into fanaticism, imagination into superstition, authority into clericalism and literalism. Furthermore, the intellect is needed to analyse and systematize the materials of religious conceptions and to investigate their history. Religion cannot stop with merely isolated facts and experiences. It must needs seek continuity and unity. Religion does not content itself with unquestioning acceptance of that which is handed down in the scriptural tradition. Religion seeks to grasp the history of revelation in its concrete reality and renews itself in contact with this concrete reality. Many of the great religious personalities have been famous thinkers, logicians, critics, scientists and scholars. We have but to name Origen, Augustine, Thomas Aquinas, Wycliffe, Calvin, Pascal, Schleiermacher, Kierkegaard, Newman, Harnack, Al Ghazali, Nagarjuna, Sankara.

Error and confusion result, however, when the role of intellect is changed from that of control to that of source of knowledge. Its role as controlling, bringing order, criticizing, systematizing, is a restricted one, but is a great and indispensable one. We must not change it to one of being a source of knowledge, of being a real revelation. It is true that even in primitive religion the intellectual search for the ultimate cause seems to lie behind the conception of the All-Father. Natural religion, so-called, rests on the supposition that the understanding must conclude from the nature of the universe the existence of God. But even if this could be done, which I doubt, there would be no real religion until other elements are added.

To human reason we may concede a part greater or less, to play in the knowledge of God. There is found today and there has been found in the past in theological and ecclesiastical thought a view which holds that a normal person, using his understanding, by observing the workings of natural law and the order of the world, must necessarily by the compulsion of logic arrive at the conclusion that there is a Creator and that He is at work in the world. We know that Aristotle had this confidence in the powers of the intellect. After him we find it in the Roman theology developed under his influence, and especially in the great Thomas Aquinas of the Middle Ages. We find it later in evangelical thought, in the theologians of Deism and of the Enlightenment. The Pope has now made Thomas Aquinas the normative theologian of the Roman Church. It now belongs to Roman Catholic orthodoxy, as a Roman Catholic theologian has succinctly phrased it, to hold the first and second articles of the creed, not as affirmations of faith but as conclusions of the reason. Plato, Augustine, Occam, Luther, with modern evangelical theology, assign a far more modest role to the human understanding. According to their view faith and the religious experience and revelation are of far greater importance in attaining certainty of God and his works.

All knowledge includes an element of will. The interest, and consequently the desire of an enquirer is directed toward the object of knowledge. When we examine an object and desire to know it, this means that, in a certain degree, we wish to possess it spiritually. This quality, which inheres more or less in all knowledge, is given an incomparably greater importance in that kind of knowledge which we call religious faith. Faith lays hold of God and holds to God, or rather, opens the way for the will and work of God and receives the love of God revealed in Jesus Christ. Faith is thus not a lesser degree of knowledge, as if, for example, one would say, I believe that the forests of northern Sweden are more beautiful than others, but I do not know whether they are. Rather, faith differs from other knowledge in its object. Faith is knowledge of the spiritual world. It differs from other knowledge in that it does not proceed from sense perceptions. Perhaps we here can apply the Hindu psychology with its doctrine of an inner sense, Manas, which perceives spiritual reality. Some have attempted to differentiate between the knowledge of faith and the knowledge of the understanding, by making the former an interested knowledge constituting a value judgement, while the latter is an uninterested, objective knowledge, an existential judgement. But this difference, as has been pointed out, is relative; the transition from one to the other is imperceptible. An element of value is found in all knowledge, and the object of faith possesses objectivity in fully as great degree as does that of knowledge based on the sense perceptions. If a comparison is to be made, it can be said that faith possesses a more certain assurance of its object than does other knowledge. For other knowledge does not possess such an all-devouring interest in its object. We could quote, in this connection, passages from Bhakti in Hinduism and Mahayana. Within the Christian church no one has more powerfully expressed the character of faith as certainty than has Martin Luther. He says of faith: "Faith receives the forgiveness of sins and makes us righteous and alive." "When the soul holds fast to the promises of God it cannot doubt that he is true, righteous, wise, and that he will act and order and care for all things in the best way. Is not such a soul, by reason of its faith, in everything most obedient to God?" Faith is more than simply a surmise or a thought. "If your conception of faith is that it is only thinking about God, then this thought can, as little as the garb of a monk, give you eternal life." Faith must consequently have its influence on the whole personality. "Faith is a certain and vital trust in the grace of God, so certain that one could die a thousand deaths on it. And this trust and knowledge of God's grace makes a man bold, joyful and at peace with God and all created things. This the Holy Spirit works through faith. By faith a man becomes willing and disposed to do good to all without constraint, to serve and to suffer all things to please God who has shown so much grace toward him."

Melanchton understood this correctly when he wrote, in the Apology for the Augsburg Confession, 1531, as follows: "Such a faith which has courage to trust in God, in life or in death, such a faith alone creates a Christian man."

We must consequently posit as the subject of faith, not the understanding, the human organ of knowledge only, but the whole spiritual being of man, which Pascal calls the heart. And if we wish to define more closely the powers of soul, the gifts or drives in man, which set faith in motion to seek God, we must necessarily come to consciousness of the infinite which we possess, consciousness of the spiritual reality which is beyond, which does not permit itself to be enclosed within measurable limits. And as another generating impulse to faith, we note the longing of man for perfection, his sense of lack, and of sin and guilt, and his striving to attain to realization of the ideal. Revelation, that is to say, God and his works, cannot be grasped by man otherwise than by faith. Faith cannot be satisfied with anything less than God himself, as he has revealed himself.

The sources of revelation, or better still, its channels through which it comes to meet faith on the part of man, are two: the *consciousness of infinity* and the *urge to the ideal*. In one sense religion and revelation are universal, for they are found in some measure in all human beings. But in another sense they are particular. They are found only in individuals

in whom the consciousness of infinity and the longing for the ideal have come to such definite form and
found such clear content, that they have been able
to satisfy and gather about them numbers of those
in humankind who hunger after salvation.

II

An obscure passage in the book of Ecclesiastes
seems to mean that "God has put eternity into the
heart of man." Whether this is the correct interpretation of the passage or not, it is nevertheless true. Many
modern thinkers, as for example, C. P. Tiele, Louis
Pasteur, F. von Hügel, would go so far as to make the
consciousness of infinity the very basis of religion in
man. There is found in man a perception which
cannot be explained by what the eyes see and the
ears hear. And perhaps Pasteur is right when he believes that the perception of the infinite is the most
certain of all human perceptions. It introduces the
soul into a higher world than the material, where
the soul can breathe more deeply and freely. The
heroes of the religion of infinity have won an eternally abiding home for thousands and thousands of
noble and devoted souls. No one can read their

writings without feeling that this infinite world, so distant from our outward world, possesses a reality, a power, a fascination. There is found a redemption and a refuge for the human spirit. In two instances in history the perception of the infinite world has brought forth types of religion which have gained significance in world-history. To be sure they have not lacked ethical elements, the passion to realize ideals of conduct, but the controlling power has been the sense of the infinite. Not always has this been pure and unmixed, but nevertheless it has been the dominant element. From India I would cite the name of Yajnavalkya, one of the great names of the Upanishads, as representative of an obscure beginning which developed into movements of vast influence with continuance in Brahmanic and Buddhistic doctrines of redemption. In the West Plotinus is the great systematizer and mystic of the consciousness of infinity. He is the perfecter of Orphism and Platonism and was himself more or less normative of the mystical currents in Christianity and in the Islam of Persia. The Aryan spirit has given the longing for infinity its greatest depth and widest range. If one is an enthusiast for an Aryan or an Indo-Germanic form of piety, undoubtedly the religion of infinity

here offers its best claim to being true-born. I use
the term consciousness of infinity because, in my
opinion, the mystical has a point of contact in every
human being. The fact that contemplation and ecstasy and the blessed experience of union with God
characterize the life of comparatively few persons
depends on certain psychical predispositions and experiences in life and also, in some measure, on particular training and preparation. I must include in
this brief paragraph concerning consciousness of infinity my conviction that visions, contemplation, do
convey to mystically gifted men and women a real
perception of the being of God. We sometimes speak
of a sixth sense with which the mystic perceives the
true reality hidden behind the world of phenomena.
Whatever explanation we may offer for such unusual and remarkable conditions of the soul's life, it
must be held true that they are related to feelings
and experiences which, in some measure, every person possesses who has been awakened to the existence of spiritual realities.

III

The urge to ideals of conduct, or conscience, is

concerned with a different kind of contrast between man and God than is the consciousness of infinity. If I may thus express it, the difference is one more purely qualitative. The decisive thing here is not the distance of the finite from the Infinite, the difference between the lowliness of man and the exaltation of God, between the noisy unrest of life and the stillness and peace of the eternal world. It is rather the difference between that which *is,* with all its lack, its inadequacy, its sin, and that which *ought to be,* perfection, realization, holiness. The longing for the ideal is revealed in the disturbance that conscience feels over the breach of certain rules of conduct. But it is deepened and intensified so that it finally becomes a burning passion for righteousness and purity, which reaches far beyond every outward regulation. It grows into an unending craving and yearning for perfection, which reveals the intimate connection which exists between the consciousness of infinity and the impulse to the ideal. In this latter I wish to point out three stages which have been of great significance in the history of religion. First there is the ideal in the form of rules and ordinances which express the ethical demands of God and of his nature. Second, there is the ideal (with also the conception of Deity) found in the form of a human person, a saint, a hero, an avatar, an incarnation, above all in Christ, whom one is compelled so far as possible to imitate. The customs of the Prophet and his immediate followers is made the object of imitation in Islam, and the imitation of Christ is the goal of St. Francis and of Roman Catholicism. Finally there is the stage on which there is present an ideal and a conception of God which cannot be expressed in rules or qualities of character, nor does it consist strictly in the life of a person to be imitated, but in the spirit, which flows from the person and work of Christ. The pursuit of the ideal is directed beyond all that which is human and seeks its footing in a transmundane, a Divine goodness. At four junctures in the history of religions has the urge to ideals brought forth or liberated significant formations, not entirely apart from the consciousness of infinity but nevertheless predominating over it. In China there was Laotse, in Iran Zoroaster, in Greece Socrates, and in Israel Moses—perhaps even Abraham. One is impressed in each of these cases with a spirit which is different from that produced by the consciousness of infinity, as the channel through which the revelation of the being of God has broken through into humanity. Perhaps the difference comes to light most clearly through a comparison of Socrates and Plato. The former is characterized by his faithfulness to conscience and his confident trust in Divine providence, the latter by his exalting yearning. Nowhere, however, does the ethical zeal of God burn away all other elements and interests in revelation as in Moses and those who followed him. The good news of Christ is a message of the Divine authority, of infinite seriousness and love.

My thesis is this: In these two, the consciousness of infinity and the urge to the ideal, the wellsprings of religion flow forth upon the earth out of the innermost depths of the Divine being. God reveals himself to us. Faith receives this revelation. In both there is a movement from the merely subjective to the objective, from the religious structure of the mind to the faith which is called forth by revelation. We are all more or less musically gifted—or at least, we will suppose that such is the case. Something of the life of music lives in all of us. But when Bach and Beethoven arise they become for us, not merely two persons much more musically gifted than the rest of us but rather, they are revelations of music itself. In them the spirit of music comes forth to

meet us. I am almost as certain that we reach in
Bach, in principle, the highest point in music, and
that Plotinus constitutes the perfection of the mysticism of infinity, as I am that Christ will never be
surpassed nor even equalled in the history of Divine
revelation. Of course this can have no demonstration
logically.

It is much the same in religion. We all possess the
sense of infinity and the longing for righteousness.
We need make no exceptions here, as in the case of
music. We all possess some share of the religious
life. We are none of us excluded from the life of the
spirit, the Spirit of God. But in some individuals
the Spirit of God breaks forth with such mighty
power that they become for us the revealers of
God. In them God comes to meet us. When we see
them we see something of God—even though no
one of them can, in the same sense with Jesus, say:
"He that hath seen me hath seen the Father." These
mirror in their character something of the power
and love of God. Luther held that each one of us
was to be a Christ to other men.

We observe here a peculiar difference between the
religion which preferably perceives the Divine under
the aspect of infinity and that in which the reality

of conscience predominates. In three respects this difference emerges, in respect to personality, to history and to authority. Other important differences must here be left to one side. In the very nature of things religion of infinity is indifferent toward personality and history. It flees from the concrete, from the complexity of this life and the chain of events, one following upon another, to the all-embracing mystery of the eternal world. But that religion which is born of and is nurtured by the longing for the ideal must concentrate in the personal life. For in the personal life only can that eye in the human soul which is called the imperative ideal recognize God and his revelation. And if the being of God is something which can be surmised by us at least approximately and can be expressed in the symbols of ethical self-realization and life-generating, redeeming, forgiving love, then the great drama of the human race must bear traces of this. In other words, history must in some sense be the epic of the Divine will. The religion of the compelling power of ideals must necessarily draw history and the personal life within the area of revelation and find in these the revelation of God—while, on the other hand, the consciousness of infinity may, I do not say *must,* but may, according to its nature, be indifferent to human history and its personalities.

In consequence the question of authority will assume, in some degree, a different form in each. I mean the question of that authority which is able to give to religion its bearing and its strength. We can see this within Christianity, when religion has risen up out of its age of childhood and can no longer content itself with an outward authority, the dictation of a hierarchy or of the letter, or of a church majority. Mysticism, influenced by Platonism and Neo-Platonism has, in such a crisis, preferably fled away to its own ethereal regions, hid in its esoteric truth, unconcerned about every authority, lost in its own visions. On the other hand, a St. Paul, an Augustine, a St. Birgitta, a Luther, a Pascal, a Bunyan, a Kierkegaard, have transferred the authority to the person of Christ and bound it to the glorified figure of Christ, of His faith, His heart and mind. It is clear that creative, revealing personalities must have as such a wholly different significance for the pursuit of ideals than for the longing for infinity.

Revelation signifies that God makes himself felt, that the divine shimmers through the earthly medium. I maintain that the eyes through which humanity views the divine are two, the longing for infinity and the urge to the ideal. Both are valuable, in normal cases they are joined. But at times it is the one and at times the other which determines the soul's conception of God. In its great personalities the longing for infinity exalts above all and reveals to us the divine world of reality far above the petty cares and the narrow limits of this world. But in order that this exaltation shall not dissolve the Divine there must be added the passion for the ideal, the hunger and thirst after an immeasurable transformation and exaltation of life. This passion courageously thrusts itself forward and achieves the impossible, becomes certain of the reality of this other world, certain of God's own nature in its positive and overwhelming majesty and power.

Where? In Nature, in the movements of the worlds, in the flow and development of life? Yes, but only dimly, doubtfully. In order to see it there, revelation must first have taken place and been appreciated within the more intimate area, in conscience and in history. No one has better expressed this than the Swedish hymn writer, J. O. Wallin. Having sung of the power, wisdom and majesty of God proclaimed by a thousand tongues in Nature, he continues:

> "But still, Thy heart I could not trace,
> Thy purpose hidden lay,
> A mite in endless realms of space,
> Adrift I sought my way.
>
> On Sinai dawned the light at last,
> On Tabor came full day.
> My soul saw clear, the darkness past,
> Thy law, Thy will revealed.
>
> Earth's anguish gained a meaning clear,
> In Heav'n's revealing light;
> Celestial voices sang their cheer,
> Heard deep in human hearts."

This is the road which revelation has taken; this way it travels at all times. Nowhere else, however, is the certainty of the nature of God, as it is achieved by an intense passion to attain perfection, stronger than it is in the person of Jesus. In no other personality has this certainty in a more effective way penetrated the whole being. No one is therefore a revelation of God in the same sense as Jesus. In no one does the Divine shine through as brightly as in him. It is not an arbitrary thing that we turn to him. One may ask, why just to him? The history of religion answers: There is for the resolve to attain the ideal no other choice. The effects of his life are such that they mark for him a central and unique place. Yet the development of his own personality and its influence is dependent essentially on the fact that he did not stand isolated. He is linked in the series of interpreters of the certainty of God, in a history which is more than typical, a history which as none other is freighted with revelation. These interpreters, the great figures of the passion for righteousness who lived before the day of Jesus, with those of our own day as well, and he himself above all, these persons, and this history appear to us as a revelation in a unique sense. The motives, the powers, the conflicts have been in no other history by the actors themselves so clearly defined, lived through and made use of in the same manner as by the prophets in the Biblical history. The prophets and their followers have become martyrs for the faith in the God of history. I do not necessarily mean by this that any orthodoxy has condemned their faith as heresy. But their insistence on an ethical core in history has brought them into an attitude of tragic inner tension even if it has not led them to physical suffering and death. These martyrs of history bring their faith to victory.

Let no one at this point call attention to the infinitely small scale of the Biblical history as compared with all that has transpired on our earth, and the infinitely small proportions of the whole of human history as compared with that of the universe. My answer to the former objection is, that science must necessarily be empirical. It cannot concern itself with that which we beforehand hold probable. Perhaps there ought to be found another history as enlightening concerning the will of God as is the Biblical history. Perhaps there ought to be found revealers as remarkable as Christ. But in fact there are none. Science must take the actual, strange as it may be, and take it seriously. The answer to the latter objection of the insignificance of the human world in the vast expanse of space, is, that when we seek for principles, essence and content, bulk does not overawe us. It is a purely relative thing whether I measure with the millionth of a millimetre or with a billion kilometres. In our experience reality is revealed in a more intensive and exalted form in human life than anywhere else in the universe.

Read, investigate, weigh carefully all that relates to this question! Some doubt may possibly arise as to which is to have the preference, consciousness of infinity or the urge to the ideal. There are those of our contemporaries who prefer the mysticism of infinity with the unity which it seeks. But if we value more the passion to attain the ideal, if we see in the impact of the Divine will on life, in the purposefulness of existence a stronger power for salvation and a richer future blessing vouchsafed the soul and the human race than is offered in a religion which catches only a glimpse of the divine in a far-off, peaceful stillness, in refuge from the temporal and the historical, then there is no doubt that in the life of Christ and in the history in which that life is set, we have the revelation of God *par préférence* within humanity, enduring and not to be surpassed. In his life and in this history, if anywhere, the cold crust of the earthly life is broken through and the warming, glowing, consuming fire of the Divine Spirit breaks forth, active ever as the Spirit of the risen Lord. Christ and the Biblical history, however, do not become truly a revelation until the veil has been taken from our eyes and we are led to see the Divine life, the will of God beneath all of existence. If we have put our whole being into this undertaking, if we have sounded the depths through our own effort and meditation, we shall be conscious of this Divine life and will in our own inner life. We shall also see it revealed in that human history in which we ourselves stand fighting and suffering. It shall be revealed to us in the phenomena of Nature, in the development of life below the level of the human, perhaps also in the changes and the laws of inorganic nature.

How can the coherence, in which science believes and which it finds present in all that exists and all that happens, how can this become a revelation to us, a testimony to the living God, to the reality of the divine will? Nearest at hand lies the expedient of translating the causal connection into purpose. The view is lifted to the future. That which happens is not simply the result of causes, but also points to an end. For example, I am walking aimlessly through a crowd, partly pushed on by those behind me, partly myself seeking a way out into the open. Just then I meet a person, and that meeting becomes decisive for my life. This event I necessarily ascribe to a purposeful guidance, an end. Another example. Concurring events bring me into a situation which I bitterly lament. Years later I bless it as something which served a purpose unknown at the time. Again, science depicts the history of Israel merely as a causal continuity leading up to the appearance of Jesus. Faith sees in this history a preparation for the great goal, Christ. Again, science studies the laws of heredity. If we only knew all the factors—which is impossible—we could, out of the many genealogies, derive that combination which resulted in the spiritual endowment of Gustavus Vasa, the founder of the modern Swedish state. It is clear to us that he was the man who was predetermined and equipped for his task.

Such transitions from causality to teleology have their validity within certain limits. But objections arise against viewing the problem of revelation as solved by permitting those generalizations, which we call the laws of Nature, to become valid as the will of God. The continuity of reality concealed from us is one thing; our generalizations and the "laws of Nature" are another.

1. We must be on our guard against a teleological

explanation in the style of the meditations of the cat on the fact that birds have wings, which of course deprives the hungry cat of her food, perhaps at the very instant when her claws are about to grasp it. This causes vexation of spirit for the cat. She finds the world order unjust, but solves the difficulty by nourishing the hope of a millennium, when birds will no longer have wings. This parable comes to my mind, a reminiscence from a book by Östrup on cats, whenever I hear pious teleological reasonings, which drag the secrets of the soul with its diabolical temptations and its comforting celestial visions of struggling faith down to the level of a shabby utilitarianism.

2. Still more serious is another difficulty. Causality sometimes turns out to be the most cruel lack of purpose. Shall we then be comforted by the hope that this also shall at last receive a satisfactory explanation in a higher light? This hope does not satisfy. Revelation is not to be found in a translation of causal continuity nor in a new insight into its meaning. Revelation is *a struggle against resisting forces.* Within all areas of life we discover plainly the contrast between that dull, dead thing, which hinders and chokes progress and itself falls prey to

dissolution, and that vital power, which is forever striving forward, always nearly overcome but yet always unwearied and conquering. On the higher levels this contrast is acute. There is something in that which happens both within and without the human world which drags down and hinders. God's continuing creation, an ever continuing creation, is also a continuing struggle. I can see what a contradiction this means for the search after a unified world view. I am also fully conscious of the imperfections in the attempt of our thought to comprehend and express the ways of reality and the life of God. It is clearer than ever to me that dualism—not an absolute dualism, but one with hope and certainty of the attainment of unity—more accurately than monism reproduces reality the more deeply we penetrate into its very life. Anyone who has been rocked to sleep in monism has never felt "the depths of Satan." I do not begrudge him his escape. But he cannot claim the right to speak as an interpreter of life.

Rather than a translation of causality into teleology, I would commend another view. We are confronted by two different planes, the plane of science and the plane of revelation. In both we are concerned in some sense with reality. In science it is, however, in a very abstract way. That is to say, our knowledge gathers up out of reality that which can be arranged within the causal continuity and such as constitutes the condition necessary for the adaptation of Nature to our purposes. Of course this scientific view of the totality with its hypotheses stands in an intimate relation with reality. The two planes do not lack connection the one with the other. But the task of science is not simply theoretical, not simply to know, but to rule. The plane of revelation is different. Here we penetrate deeper than we are able to do with the intellect alone. Here we must throw ourselves, for life or death, into a wrestling with reality itself. We discover that we certainly are not the conquerors. If we are to experience the restoring power we must realize that we are completely defeated. If we are to find a revelation we must seek for and we must discover something solid on which to build. It is not a question of an intellectual game, nor of an investigation which possesses only practical significance and whose criterion of truth is practical utility. On the contrary, we seek to penetrate into and to catch the message of reality itself. The truth is that God himself presses in upon us.

We can as I have shown in a number of examples,

superimpose the plane of science upon the plane of revelation and seek to express the matter thus: God works through the laws of Nature. But essentially the two views serve different purposes. The so called laws of Nature do not give us the essence of reality. No critical scientist believes that reality consists of the ether or the atoms, but we know well, professional scientists and others, that God is the true reality.

Certainty of the living God we gain, as did the prophets and the apostles, by an experience of communion with the life of God. The more wholeheartedly we can devote ourselves to reality, that is, to the demands which life makes on us to repent and to obey, either in fiery efforts or in quiet self-dedication and rest, the more certain are we to gain and to retain the conviction that God does exist and that he is an unfathomable Goodness, fighting his way through and that he is able to carry us through. If we are strictly conscientious and exacting we must admit that we are not able to perceive much of the revelation of God. In every case, this is our fault, not God's. Still, we know that we have met him in our life, we are conscious as we look back upon life, of his guidance. History unveils for us at times God's way of dealing. In a situation which appears without comfort or help there shines through it all a sense of the purpose of God,—shall we dare to lay hold on it and believe in it? We must believe, in spite of all! We must hope against all hope! If the mere event as a dead thing rises up before us and obscures our view of revelation, we must go to the Bible. There heaven is open and its light penetrates through the grey mists and fearful darkness of our life.

Only as we pray and labour are we able to hold fast the revelation. The mystic speaks of a purification, a *via purgativa*, which constitutes the first rung of the ladder to heaven upon which he seeks to reach the Divine life. To this purification belongs the ethical life of man and its development. In reality the connection between the moral life of man and his communion with God is closer than this. Only as active champions for the eternal goodness in ourselves and others do we create within us that attitude in which we can truly commune with God. That man has little or no need of questioning concerning the existence and work of God who prays and labours with soul and body in the power of his prayer. "If any man willeth to do his will, he shall know of the teaching, whether it be of God, or whether I speak of myself." No one can possibly doubt the existence of That One, with whom he communes earnestly and with greater interchange than with any human being. "In Him we live and move and have our being." He is our life.

III

CONTINUED REVELATION

*A Contribution to the Interpretation of the Belief in
Revelation, throwing Light on the General History of Religion and Christian Theology*

I

IN CERTAIN of the later writings of the Old
Testament and in Judaism, piety no longer discerns the activity of God in the historical events and
personalities of the present. It is more likely to be
found in the wise and magnificent order of Nature.
In history it is found only in the ancient miracles of
revelation. By reason of the place which Christ was
given in the Christian's communion with God,
Christianity finds itself in a different situation re-
garding faith in revelation. A certain likeness is
found, however, *mutatis mutandis*, between the Judaism which retained the certainty of revelation only
in that which happened long ago, and the average
Protestant conception, according to which the revelation of God is a finished product of antiquity and
written down in its entirety in the Holy Book.

140

"And God said unto Moses." So ran the lesson in
Bible history a boy was reading aloud as he studied.
His younger, more rationalistically inclined brother
interrupted him with the words: "But God cannot
speak to human beings in that manner." The school
boy knew the right answer: "Hush, He could in
those days."

Into this view there is woven a bit of inalienable
Christian conviction. Revelation is a thing at hand,
completed once for all in Jesus Christ and since his
day needs not to be remade or improved. John records the words of Jesus concerning the Spirit: "He
shall take of mine, and shall declare it unto you."
Christ, who suffered under Pontius Pilate, the Christ
of history, in the light of faith is valid for all time.
The history, which is related in the Bible, constitutes
the revelation of God in a fuller, richer, weightier
sense than that of any other history. The unique
revelatory quality of the history recorded in the Bible
appears impossible and unbelievable to apriori reasoning, but receives to a certain extent a surprising
confirmation in the comparative study of religions,
when this science has had sufficient time to find its
bearings in the confusing abundance of its material.[1]

---

[1] Cf. Chapter II, and also my article, "Communion with Deity," in
Hastings's *Encyclopædia of Religion and Ethics*.

For history is not made according to the laws of logic. What one finds there may be quite absurd, indeed, one would say beforehand, that it is unthinkable. But still, it has happened. It is material for scientific investigation, which must in this case, as always, in order to reach genuine results, take its position beneath its object of investigation, listening, absorbing, interpreting; not above its object in an attitude of domination. In the history of religion there is revealed a supernatural life, but not always what human thought might esteem just and correct. As we have sought to show earlier in this book, the actual appearance of the history of religion agrees with the words of St. Paul about a general revelation, within which we can discern a special revelation. Or, to use terms which do not have any metaphysical import, within the religion of the race appear certain phenomena, which in a special sense deserve the name revealed religion. To show, however, how impossible it is to hold that there is in truth such a divine revelation and at the same time to hold that it is concluded for all time in Christ and the Bible, it is necessary only to combine two questions: "Does God continue to reveal himself to humanity?" and: "Has God ever revealed himself to humanity?" The latter question lies threateningly behind the former and shows how impossible it is to maintain that there is a true revelation unless we assume that it continues in the present time. How can we convince a man who does not believe that there is a divine influence, and for whom there exists no living God, that a God really exists, who at one time revealed himself to man, if God does not now reveal himself to that man as living and redeeming him? And yet there are Christians, who believe in God, not simply as a law or principle, a great, all-penetrating mystery, but as a will and as love which has made itself known to man, and yet maintain that revelation closed with Christ and the Bible. The following discussion is therefore intended as a contribution toward the further development of the Christian idea of revelation. I call attention to a continuing divine self-impartation, which manifests itself as a creating power and a redeeming will. Most clearly this is shown in three areas of life, in Nature, in history and in the moral life. These may be further defined by three phenomena: 1) genius as a phase of nature, 2) the continuity and purposiveness of history, 3) the regeneration of the individual and the formation of character. If this continued revelation takes place within Christendom it marks the continued action of Christ. Belief in and experience of his living power is the identifying characteristic common to all Christianity.

The theologians of Pio Decimo and Professor Wilhelm Herrmann were agreed upon one point: God has revealed himself in Jesus Christ. But at once their ways parted. In more recent evangelical thought there has emerged a conception of revelation, which because of its concentration assumes a position as solid as rock and as hard as diamond. It is the conception that revelation does not consist in any individual events or any statements or writings. It consists in the inner life of Christ in relation to the Father and in his love, so divinely fixed and powerful. If, however, one has met God in Christ, one can no longer isolate Christ. The man who says: "God is revealed in Christ," at the same time says: "God is revealed in Nature." The man who says: "God is revealed in Christ," cannot escape saying: "God is revealed in history."

The ancient Church used the term "nature" concerning Christ. However anxious the theology of our time may be to observe and to preserve continuity with that which the Church at that time pro-

nounced as a postulate of faith: Two natures, one
divine, the other human, it must nevertheless, today,
take other aspects of the matter for its investigation
and express the being of the Saviour in other terms.
Do we consider the Divine to be a nature? Is there
a nature which is specifically super-animal or human? What we call nature, is it really nature conceived in the ancient manner as substance? In recent
times another distinction has been made as to the
person of Christ. Modern theology draws a line between nature and character, between that in Jesus
which was given, inherited, "natural," just as in any
human being, and that which was the product of
his will, his self-discipline, that is, his ethical personality, his character, the seriousness and purity of
love and righteousness in him, that which we call
the ethical and spiritual life in any human being.
Under the influence of its heritage from pietism and
rationalism, modern theology has viewed the saving
power of Christ as residing in his ethical perfection
and mighty love. Such a view means indeed an advance in the apprehension of Christ and of revelation. But is it satisfactory? Let us ask from a purely
empirical and historical standpoint: "What elements
in the person of Christ constitute his unparalleled

religious significance, according to the testimony of history?" I do not now refer to the uniqueness of the historical situation or to other religio-historical circumstances, concerning which we shall have occasion to speak in another paragraph in this chapter. The answer is naturally, his spiritual and moral greatness, the intense seriousness of his will, his divinely passionate mercy, his powerful intuition of personal truth. Certainly, these are the most important elements. But can we stop with these? Take any foundation-laying personality, prophet or great saintly figure that you will, can his influence be explained solely by his ethical glory and his supreme goodness? No indeed. Behind him lies Nature—in his mighty endowments. He has not created himself. From whence has he come? In a sermon written in 1544 Luther asks: "St. Peter, St. Paul, Augustine, Ambrosius, John Huss, I myself, Dr. Martinus, from whence have all these come?" Had he been ever so holy and determined, could Pascal have accomplished what he did or attained to the place he holds in the kingdom of God, if he had not been born into this world with the exquisite and powerful gifts we all admire in him? And these were his without any of his own doing. In an immensely greater degree this holds true of Christ. My objection is, that we seek to understand the deity of Christ only on the basis of his truth, his holiness and love, without taking into account the treasures of his incomparable gifts, which lay hidden already in the womb of Mary—that is, without reckoning with the revelation of God in Nature and through Nature. That Jesus became the Saviour of the world was due, not only to his moral greatness but, in the first place, to the mystery of the endowment which was his from birth, to the Incarnation. "The Word became flesh." The revelation is given, not alone in the holiness of Christ, but also in the miracle of his nature, of his human blood. One could add, that the close union between natural gifts and ethical power often puts to a severe test our longing to see righteousness established in the world order. To find anything like an illuminating comparison or point of contact for the interpretation of the person of Christ, it is clear that we must turn to the extraordinary personalities in history. Any view of the deity of Christ, which cuts off every connection with these, is as much contrary to the dogma as to the gospel.

The emergence of *genius* is in its way a constant demonstration of the truth that the essence of reality is creation, the eternal creation of something new, not a dead connection of cause and effect. Or, in other words, the inner compulsion which lies behind that which is visible to our eyes and audible to our ears, is a necessary urgency to create, to generate, to save, to make alive, to bring forth something new out of the hidden treasures of being. It is not a mechanical necessity, which simply administers and in new ways combines that which is already at hand. In the phenomenon of genius there breaks forth a mighty wave of creative power. It is clear to us, that the genesis of genius follows determined laws. Many genealogies lie behind the child, in whose unborn body lie slumbering wondrous treasures. Inheritance, dangerous inheritance, good inheritance, weak inheritance, through thousands of changes of heredity in its forebears, produces differing results. A combination and a reciprocal influence come from the talents of father and mother, but not from them only, but also from earlier inheritances. The parents pass these on from the generations before them in a mysterious way to the individual or individuals, who after them take over the hidden possibility for good or for evil. This the parents often do without having themselves benefited from their values or suffered from their weight. The endowment of genius itself usually breaks forth to all appearance as suddenly and as much unmediated as the biological phenomenon, which since deVries has been called mutation, a term which aims to express the inexplicable in the affair. In lower organisms, in plants and the lower orders of animals, remarkably keen analyses have been made of the conditions of heredity. Certainly there are hidden laws of heredity, which can be in part discovered by scientific investigation. Innumerable facts and details in previous generations must be taken into account in seeking an explanation of the suddenness and mysteriousness with which genius emerges before men's eyes. No mere process of addition of lofty and refined qualities will yield such a result. The riddle of generation and heredity is more complex than any sum in addition. We shall never be able fully to analyse the sources of a creative spirit and the constitutive elements in it. But we believe and know in all of higher culture, that there is no such thing as chance, nothing merely happens, there is no break in the chain of real connection, although human eyes cannot penetrate the series of causes and effects. The Christian faith and the synthetic view of life and history also know something more. They know that God works in the complex connections of the generations and that the right man is found at hand to perform his work when he is needed. Alas, it seems necessary again to emphasize that our line of thought is not concerned with the manner in which genius suddenly emerges. Its sudden, puzzling character is due to our imperfect analysis of the sequence of the generations. We are here concerned with the character of genius itself, with the results, not the method. In a measure it is true of every human being that it possesses in its being something original and unique, which is not fully like any other. Geijer has given us a word which is not only one of the most comforting that have been spoken, but also one of the truest. He says that there does not exist a person who cannot do some one thing better than any one else. In creative genius, however, the new and the unique is revealed more clearly than in others. The phenomenon of creative spirits make us surmise that life in its reality is a continuing creation, not simply an administration.

Genius pursues one way of working, whatever may be the material with which it works. This material may be the hearts of men, states, armies, tones, colours, figures, fabrics, words. Language has with sure instinct fixed on the word which describes what is done with this material. It is creation. Something new emerges, something original, not found before. It is not always easy to determine wherein the new thing consists. But the fact that it is new distinguishes the work of genius from that of the merely talented. We can see this distinction more clearly if we but note the fact that the work of talent, be it ever so remarkable, but still merely talent, consists in a skilful reproduction according to rules and patterns. The work of genius, however, gives rise to new rules, which analysis afterwards discovers. *Creation* comes first, in revelation, in beauty of character, in social structure, in the work of art. Afterwards comes *doctrine,* in theology, in ethics, in theory of government, in theory of art. Exactly as in nature, the world of God's material creation; first flowers, then botany. Genius emerges as an essential element in the continuing creation of the Almighty. Genius is often also conscious of participation in a miracle. Plato knew that those who were inspired uttered words, the meaning of which they themselves were unable to grasp. Harald Hjärne has said: "Not all seers are able to interpret their own visions." History verifies this observation. God alone knows the interpretation. Coming generations never tire of seeking to penetrate more and more deeply into the works of genius and of drawing from them constantly new instruction and edification. There is for us professors, a very healthy warning in the paradox, that great men are always right even when they contradict one another.

Having said this, however, the entire meaning of the creative work of genius has scarcely even been hinted at. Genius possesses another aspect even more wonderful, to which attention is seldom called. Perhaps I may call this the organic connection between the continuing creation of God and the work of men of genius. *Men of genius are the appointed interpreters of God's creation.* Existence is difficult to interpret and easily appears meaningless, bitterly meaningless. Through their powers of penetration, through their personalities and their creations, men of genius aid us to see or to surmise a meaning in life. This they do, not merely as thinkers. No, not primarily as thinkers, but as doers, as heroes, martyrs, prophets, saints, as artists, inventors, composers, poets. Their unique endowment reveals thus a mysterious connection with creation itself. Let me

illustrate with a very humble example. We say, perhaps with a bit of merry snobbishness: "This sunset
is like a picture of this or that painter." And it is
really so, for before him and without him no one
ever saw the same glory and the same colours. Why
is it that for thousands of years Europeans saw no
beauty in a wild mountain landscape? It is only in
the last one hundred and fifty years that men have
seen it. Luther journeyed through Switzerland twice
without seeing the Alps, and yet he had ordinarily
keen eyes to see the beauty of nature. Rousseau and
Romanticism taught the Western world the glory of
the Alps. In China and Japan the beauty of the
snow-capped mountains had been appreciated far
earlier. But in both cases it was genius which revealed the matter, that is, interpreted God's creation.
Genius points the way; afterwards it is as easy as
Columbus's egg. Something similar is revealed in
the far more important areas of life. As regards po-
etic and artistic genius the matter has been expressed
by Geijer in the following words: "Humanity has a
hard and laborious way to traverse. Goals and rules
constitute what we call the divine order. His plan
God has hidden in his divine wisdom, but he has
given it to his most beloved creatures to study as a

school exercise, a problem to meditate upon and to solve. This task is now proceeding in a strange and fragmentary manner, as it appears to our eyes, and there would be faint hope of the task ever being successfully finished, were it not for the fact that the Schoolmaster has his hand in the matter. The thought is for us awe-inspiring that the very idea of order would be lost, if it could be proved only by the outward reality. Faith certainly fixes its eye on the goal, but sees only in part. It discerns perhaps no more than the golden cross which surmounts the spire of the temple. Science searches for the ground plans, but its work is also fragmentary. Therefore God has placed along this long and toilsome road of humanity's progress persons who possess the unique ability to bring forth for our reflection, out of their own inner life, in different ways and with different materials,—words, sounds, colours, proportions— *pictures* which shine with the light of God's order. Such a light of glory we call beauty, and it refreshes the heart of man."

Geijer's words show us how the *interpreter* of Creation and the *instrument* of Creation coincide with each other. Still more clear does this connection become when we come to the men of genius in history. No genius of the higher order has ever been able to content himself with finding the universe and life meaningless, and halted in materialism. In history we find a line of men of genius, who have in wider or narrower spheres created a meaning for life, when life seemed ready to dissolve in egoistic narrowmindedness and inert disintegration. Men of genius transform the situation. Life, a moment ago as empty as an empty sack or as sluggish as a full sack, awakens anew under their touch, becomes manly and alert. Powers undreamed of—Ah, were there really such powers in ordinary human beings!—gather and set themselves to the accomplishment of superhuman tasks. We know this from the history of nations. How was not all of Denmark stirred by Absalon, as later by the great Margaret! How did not life in France receive new strength and new will through Jeanne d'Arc or the Great Revolution—may the great little Virgin forgive me for classifying them together! The same thing happened in England under Elizabeth and again under Cromwell; in Sweden under Gustavus Vasa and Gustavus Adolphus; in Russia through Peter the Great; in the United States through Washington; in Germany through Bismarck. The seriousness and spiritual power in these personalities filled their epoch with meaning and sacrifice. At times we long for the return of those days to lift us out of the musty and muddy days of the present. As Carlyle writes in the introduction to the *Letters of Cromwell*: "The ancient Reign of God, for which all true men have always striven in their several dialects and modes, giving place to the modern reign of NO-God, whom men call Devil—this in its multitudinous meanings and results is a sight to create reflection in the earnest man." His desire that there should be found a history of all heroisms, means for me, that there should be found a history of the continued revelation of God. The important thing for us is that our eyes be opened to see the heroisms of our own day, and not the least, those which are demanded for the problems which lie before us in the present.

More widely and more profoundly than the men of political life go the heroes of religion. They have fought and won,—no, I should not say won—they have received on their knees a new certainty of the meaning of the ways of God. They fought for their cause and for their time, but the gain has become ours. God was with them and his Spirit operates through them still.

Melanchton, in a letter written in 1537, describes
Luther as a God-sent prophet. It is not surprising
that the sorrow at Luther's death took such forceful
expression. Dr. Jonas said in his funeral sermon at
Eisleben, that the times always were at their worst
immediately following upon the lifetime of God's
greatest men and prophets. When they passed away
terrible judgements always followed. Melanchton
gave utterance in his lectures to the following words:
"The doctrine of the forgiveness of sins and the faith
in the Son of God has not been discovered by the
subtlety of the human mind. It has come by revelation from God through this man (Luther) whom
He raised up." In his Latin funeral sermon he
points out that God's presence in the Church is at-
tested by the Lord's chosen servants, who are the
choicest flower of humanity. Bugenhagen spoke of
Luther's high office as apostle and prophet and
called to mind the prophecy of John Huss. According to Dürer, Luther was regarded by his century as
a "gottgeistig" man, a God-inspired man, foretold in
the Bible and by the prophets of the Middle Ages.
Johann Klajus from Herzberg wrote: "Just as the
Holy Spirit spoke pure Hebrew through Moses and
the prophets, and pure Greek through the apostles,

so has he spoken good German through his chosen servant, Luther." A much more authoritative testimony is given by the Formula of Concord, which not only calls Luther "the chief framer of the Confession of Augsburg" but also says that "this highly enlightened man (in the Latin text, "this hero"), endowed with the Holy Spirit's unique and highest gifts, saw in the Spirit, what should happen after his death." Older Lutheran theologians reserve for Luther in their dogmatics a special locus, which we must regard as an attempt to justify the continuance of revelation. Johann Gerhard, the greatest of the Lutheran scholastics, quotes many times the call of Luther, especially in his defence against the papal theologians. He considered the refutation of the arguments against the legitimacy and the divine plan in the raising up of Luther, as a part of the justification of the evangelical denominations as being themselves the true Catholic church.[1] At the Jubilee of 1617, he devoted a disputation to the call of Luther. In his dogmatics he touches on the matter many times and in Chapter XXVI it is discussed

---

[1] Notice the title of Johann Gerhard's *Confessio catholica, in qua doctrina catholica et evangelica, quam ecclesiae Augustanae confessioni addictae profitentur, ex Romano-catholicorum scriptorum suffragiis confirmatur*, 1634–37.

in a special section. In the chapter touching the last judgement, he denies the papal contention that Luther was a false prophet because he had said that the judgement was soon to come.[1] In the chapter concerning the Church [2] the double assertion of the Lutheran dogmatic, that Luther's call was both ordinaria and extraordinaria, is especially defended against Cardinal Bellarmine. The proofs of the former were the fact that Luther had received in a regular manner the call and the ordination to the office of priest in 1507, the validity of which was not impaired by the irregularity of the ordaining Bishop; furthermore, his degree of Doctor of Theology, with the oath which made it his duty not to proclaim heretical doctrines; and also the legal call to the professorship in Wittenberg University in 1507. As for his extraordinary call, Bellarmine held that it must be proved by miracle. Gerhard asks if it is not a miracle that a man without force of arms, with only the force of the Word and weapons of the unarmed, was able to break the supreme power in the world. For,

---

[1] *Loci theologici,* Jena 1615–23, 8 tomes, XXXI, par. 84. Cf. below page 161 f.

[2] *Loci theologici* XXV, par. 200.

Rome has dominated the world but got the Pope as Lord,
The city used force, the Pope used fraud.
Greater than both is Luther, because he, for city and
    world
Became a teacher true, by his pen alone.[1]

As regards Luther's commission to reform the Church and to reveal Anti-Christ, this consisted, according to Gerhard, in something more than the ordinary call to the Priesthood. "Although he was not called immediately of God as were the prophets and the apostles, and although he did not speak with the immediate inspiration of the Holy Spirit as they did (because of this some deny that Luther's call was extraordinary, that is, immediate), it cannot be denied that there was something extraordinary and unique in this work of reformation and the revealing of Anti-Christ." This is proved also by prophecies in the Bible, and by Luther's equipment, his powers of soul, success, etc. In chapter XXVI *De ministerio ecclesiastico,* a whole section (VIII) is devoted to the subject "Concerning the call of the blessed Luther" *("De vocatione Beati Lutheri"),* and

---

[1] Roma orbem domuit, sed Romam Papa subegit,
    Viribus illa suis, fraudibus iste suis.
    Quantum isto major Lutherus major et illa.
    Orbem urbemque uno qui docuit calamo.

along the line given above the argument is carried out in detail. It was not difficult for the theologians to find in the writings of Luther reference to his call to the gospel ministry which he had received in regular order. It is well known what a support Luther, like many others after him, found in the public obligation thus laid up on him. "I have often said," he writes, "and say it still, that I would not take all the treasure in the world for my doctorate. For I should in truth be finally disheartened and despair in the difficult matter which rests upon me if I had begun it by stealth, or of my own will, without a divine call and command. But both God and man must now give me the testimony, that I have begun it publicly in my office as doctor and preacher." Gerhard writes, that just as the priests of Jerusalem attacked the regularity of John the Baptist and of Christ (John 1:25; Matt. 21:23), just so the papal clerics now do with Luther. As we shall see in the following pages, it is by no means difficult to find also in the mouth of Luther himself very strong words about the extraordinary endowment and the task with which God had entrusted to him. But such expressions, with the exception of the prophecy of Huss, which Luther applied to himself, are not used

by John Gerhard. Quenstedt expressly states that
Luther never anywhere based his authority on any
immediate and extraordinary call.[1] He is right in
this. Luther was anxious, as were also the systematic
theologians who followed him, to validate the official regularity and continuity in his action. This
did not, however, affect the clear certainty which he
also had that he was an extraordinary instrument of
God. It is easy to understand, that the Lutheran
theologians in their defence and polemic against the
papal party would not make use of such sayings, valuable though they may be for our understanding of
Luther. Because his enemies then, even as now, interpreted them as being the utterance of an ungodly,
even a diabolical arrogance. J. Gerhard and the dog-
maticians before and after him seek proof of "the
extraordinary, even unparalleled element, which although it does not completely coincide with the immediate and entirely unique call of the apostles,"
still rises above the ordinary priestly call. They seek
this proof preferably—almost exclusively—in known
facts, only exceptionally in any strong words of
Luther about himself. Aegidius Hunnius, charac-

---

[1] *Theologia didacti-polemica, sive systema theologicum.* Wittenberg
1691, Chap. XII, 3 obs.

terized by contemporaries as "one of the chief of
those theologians who wish to be called Lutheran,"
fixed upon a term by which to designate the extraordinary element in the call of Luther, a term earlier
used about him,[1] and which Gerhard and others
adopted as expressing a position midway between
the apostles and other servants of the Church.
Luther's call is said to be "heroic *(heroica)*." Gerhard brings forward six proofs or series of proofs:
1) Predictions or prophecies in the Scriptures (Jer.
51:48; Dan. 11:44; Mal. 4:5; 2 Thess. 2:9; Rev.
14:6), and the prophecy of Huss about the rise of
Luther; 2) the outstanding and uncommon gifts of
Luther, "with which God richly and mercifully endowed his instrument for the battle against the kingdom of Anti-Christ, such as his rare learning, great
skill in languages, keenness of judgement, an almost miraculous ability to translate the Scriptures,
divine eloquence, a special power of the Spirit in almost every sentence"; 3) "Luther's heroic courage
even in the greatest of dangers"; 4) his miraculous
escape from treachery and violence; 5) his own predictions of coming events—here Gerhard refers to a
special essay on Luther's predictions and to the locus

---

[1] *Disp. 10 in Augustanam Confessionem,* according to J. Gerhard.

about the Church [1]; and 6) the remarkable progress of the Evangelical preaching unaided by worldly
power, through the Word alone. Quenstedt discusses
the same argument in his stiffly scholastic *Systema
theologicum* under the question: "Was Luther's call
to the teaching office in the Church legal and in con-
formity with the prevailing order?" [2] Among the
additional proofs, moreover, which he cites for an
extraordinary divine appointment he names the restoration of the doctrine of "justification which gives
life" and of "living words which flow out of faith,"
and also the rich spiritual hymns and glowing, ef-
ficacious prayers of Luther.

In a certain degree many of the true and great
saints of Christendom reveal in their own favoured
spirits something of the character of God himself.
They visualize for us how the Father of our Lord
Jesus Christ lives and works even until now. But of
no one, as far as my knowledge and judgement go,
is this true in higher degree than of Martin Luther,
whether one observes the originality and prophetic
meaning of his thoughts, or the freshness, the power
and richness of his personality as a testimony to the

---

[1] Par. 300, should be Par. 290.
[2] Chap. XII. quaestio III.

living presence of God. He shared with Socrates, Christ, St. Paul and the very greatest,—and we might add, with some whom we may think under mere illusion—a consciousness of his own importance. Already in 1521, in a letter of January 25 to his Elector, he called attention to the claim, that he had done everything for the salvation and blessedness of Christendom and for the good of the German nation. In 1533 he wrote in the preface to his defence against the accusation of Duke George that he incited to treason: "Such a boast and honour have I by the grace of God, that, whether the Devil and all his creatures like it or not, since the days of the apostles no doctor or writer, no theologian or jurist, has so gloriously defended, enlightened and comforted the conscience of the laity as I have done, through the special grace of God. This I know most certainly. For not even St. Augustine and St. Ambrose, although they are the best in this matter, are in these things equal to me. I boast of this with thanks and to the praise of God, and to the pain and chagrin of the Devil and all my tyrants and enemies." [1] "Of the gifts of God one should boast," he writes in another place. A superficial judgement

---

[1] E. A. XXXI, 236.

or prejudice sees in such words mere arrogance. But study the man thoroughly, observe his artless humility and note his significance in the history of religion, in the history of the revelation of God. See him battling against the hell of anguish and despair, or, again, in trusting faith "exultingly rejoice that he has a merciful God and Father, yea, resolve with a fearless and unconquerable spirit to break his way through mountains of brass and all manner of opposition and declare that all flows with honey, milk and wine; no longer mortal, but living the life eternal."[1] No one can have penetrated deeply into the man without recognizing even in his boastful words the clear understanding, such as favoured men of God have had of their call, an insight which did not make them vain.

When men of genius wholeheartedly and consciously serve God they become saints. The doctrine of the saints lost its place in evangelical theology when the cult of saints was eliminated in the name of the Gospel. I concede that the Roman church is so far right in its doctrine of the saints, that the saints are those Christians, who in an extraordinary way

---

[1] Cf. Gottschick, "Das Verhältniss von Diesseits und Jenseits in Christentum," in *Zeitschrift für Theologie und Kirche,* IX, 149.

reveal the power of God. But divine power must not be conceived of in the primitive way, as revealed in unusual acts to be classed as miracles, which many would refer to suggestion. It must rather be conceived of as acting in accordance with a Christian conception of God.[1] The meaning of the word "saint" has been distorted in different ways. Some conceive of saints as objects of cult and reverence, as though they were something in themselves. Their own testimony is that they possess nothing of themselves of which they can boast, but all is of God. I can think of no more accurate description of the saints than this: Saints are those who, in life, in spirit and in deeds, clearly and unmistakably show us that God lives. I could name saints who are living today? Or again some whose character and fellowship remain as real to us as when they were living in our circle and near us, although they have passed from the earthly scene? I do not think it necessary to cite any names. Those of us who use a little thought will find many who are truly saints.

---

[1] For *Catechismus ex decreto concilii tridentini III*, II quaestio VIII-XIV, saints are in reality objects of a cult, whose veneration and invocation must be regulated only so that the glory of God is not trespassed. For the meaning of Sanctus, see H. Delehave in *Analecta Bollandiana*, Section XXVIII, p. 145 ff. See also the essay on Saints in my *När stunderna växla och skrida*.

II

A place of honour is due those great figures of religion who have put their soul into the task of serving and seeing the will of God *in history*. I purposely use the order, *serve and see*. For in the kingdom of God no one can see so long as he remains merely a spectator. Those only who serve the will of God freely and sacrificially can see the will of God. In other affairs the order may well be that one should first look into a matter and understand it before one enters upon it. In the kingdom of God the opposite is true. Here we enter upon *history* as the second area of the continuing revelation of God. We must now turn to those who have been the first to see in history a real disclosure of God, namely, Moses and the prophets, and in some measure also the prophet of Iran, Zoroaster. Others before them have interpreted history as a mere sequence of events in the past and present. History, conceived of as purposing something higher than all merely human calculations and combinations of power,[1] leading on to

---

[1] Harald Hjärne, *Historiska världsbilder,* i Svenskt och främmande, Stockholm, 1908, pp. 147 ff.

the complete victory of God, to a rational goal, is not found expressed before the day of Moses and the prophets, nor outside of their influence. How foreign the thought of a revelation in history was for the ancient Græco-Roman world can be seen for example in Cicero. In his *De Natura Deorum* he classifies with his usual order and particularity the forms of manifestation of Divine Providence, but he does not touch upon or even intimate the thought of the presence of God in the events and connections of history. For Mosaism, on the other hand, the miracles of history were fundamental. God rescued his people out of Egypt. History proclaims his righteousness and grace. What differentiates the prophets and their kindred spirits from the saints and great personalities of other religions? The distinctive thing in all saints is that they have deeply experienced the love of God and revealed this for the good of man. The great men of other religions have sought and found God by fleeing *from history* into a timeless communion with God. The prophets commune with God *in history:* Their inner experience becomes stronger and more rich by being filled with the thought of the work of God in history. In history they hear the voice of God. It is true,

they hear other voices also. They hear the voices of
a frivolous, an unrepentant and self-sufficient people.
They see arrogance and callousness, lack of understanding and darkness, so that at times everything
looks dark to their eyes. They see the wrecks of
fallen nations. The self-sufficient nationalism of their
own people threatens to becloud every issue. The
destruction of their own nation causes bitter pain,
for it appears to them to be ethically conditioned
and inescapable. But they know also that God lives
and that he holds the reins in his hands. The identifying mark of prophetic religion, in all times, is
this: God speaks to me, to us, in history, in the small
history of the individual and in the great history of
the nation and of the world. We need not go back
to the Old Testament to find this. The greatest witness to the revelation of God in history is Jesus.

Jesus set himself as clearly as possible in dependent
relation to the past history of his people, conceived
of as the dealings of God with them. He came to
fulfil the law and the prophets, he is the Son who
follows the servants. Still more, his place in the con-
temporaneous history was that of a prophet.[1] Jesus

---

[1] Einar Billings, *De etiska tankarne i urkristendomen*, II. Upsala
1907, pp. 6 ff.

did not live in the cell of the mystics. He was a champion in the midst of confusion and battle. Jesus did not stand apart on the heights as a spectator; he mingled with the crowd of human beings, although he did often withdraw to the mountain by himself alone. Jesus won his authority for every age and for every soul, not by looking away from his age and holding himself apart from its struggles, but by going deep down into the life of his people at the definite moment in which he was placed. No people has so intensively lived its history as Israel. No personality stands more firmly set in history than is Jesus. How did he not strive for his people: "Let it stand yet another year." How did he not battle with his people for its soul: "How often have I desired to gather thy children!" If history is not the revelation of God, the struggles of Jesus are meaningless, yea, his aim one great illusion. If you wish to have Christ you must take history with him. For he stands within history bearing the fullest measure of responsibility and under the most powerful dramatic tension. The solidarity of Jesus with history is best shown in his anticipation of the immediate, catastrophic coming of the complete lordship of God. The transformation was at the door. No more important lesson has been learned by the theology of our day than the insight into this eschatological character of Christ's message. The kingdom was coming. Christ himself was to be revealed in the clouds of heaven coming in great glory before the end of his generation. There is nothing here to fear or to conceal. Christ expected a catastrophe which did not occur. On the contrary, his expectation of a speedy transformation belongs to the true humanity of Christ. This has in principle always been held by the Church. This expectation proved itself of great significance for his calling. The eschatological tension helped to compress his demands and make them firm and essential. At the same time they were thereby lifted up to an ideal height, which makes them valid beyond his own time. The moments were precious. A weak man would have shouted, hurried, run anxiously from one thing to another, or else have given up all action, sat down with folded hands to look up into heaven and to speculate with the apocalyptists as to the nature of the coming life. The strong man was calm as never before. The concentration made for a gathered power. Jesus had no time for all the unimportant nonessentials of culture. "Your heavenly Father knoweth that ye have need of these things." But he had time for all that must be done. He treated every individual case with that great conscientiousness, which alone he possesses for whom the present moment is filled with eternity. His eyes caressed lovingly the flowers of the field, his teaching reached to the heart and centre of the moral life. Furthermore, this eschatological expectation was no chance, passing thing. It is found also in many of the great figures of history. This is due not merely to the fact that the life of the individual is short and the end immediately at the door; not to the fact, which is psychologically true, that in the moment of the greatest concentration of life, death stands near us without causing us fear.[1]

Time remains brief when we stand before the

---

[1] This was written in 1911, a few years before the great war. The world catastrophe furnished an unexpected commentary on the eschatological and apocalyptic scriptures. Their seemingly fantastic scenes were given meaning. The little apocalypse found in the synoptics speaks of the final tribulation. Were we not already entered upon the beginning of the birthpangs? The drama of the apocalyptic was no longer merely a curiosity. It received life and content. The book of Revelation in the New Testament won many new readers. No other passages in the Scriptures or the sacred literature of the race could better express what men felt. Before this the eschatological and apocalyptical writings needed an apologetic. Interpreters sought to soften them, to explain away their wild and varied imagery. The comfort of civilization could not tolerate such bizarre things. But when the world-anguish had ravaged us for a time, they no longer needed interpretation. Least of all they could be explained away. (1930)

ideal, even if millions of years spread out before humanity on its march. In the midst of labours, burdened for the future, the great personalities of history have lived in an eschatological tension. Darkness closed down upon them, but within them the goal lived as a present demand and the issue as a present reality. The goal was such that no merely human progress, however long, could fulfil its meaning, but the heavenly vision was very near. For them, as for Jesus, the eschatological expectation and feeling signified, that beyond the thunders of history, and the angel voices too, they saw and heard what was in reality taking place, in spite of the present seeming bewilderment. The prince of this world was being cast out. The Son of Man was drawing all unto himself (John 12:29-32).

Belief in the continued revelation of God has since the day of the prophets created a literature characterized by one or the other of two motives, either a gloomy turning from the present to a violent catastrophe, or a more optimistic evolutionary doctrine. What is more important, the certainty that God is really the actor in the drama of history, has produced personalities, which shine with the light of God. Permit me to name some of these out of the

Christian world of Western Europe. The Church of
the Middle Ages and France possesses the most beautiful of all, Jeanne d'Arc. We have already mentioned her name. Lutheranism has Luther and Gustavus Adolphus. Calvinism has Calvin and Gaspard
de Coligny and Cromwell. History is indeed difficult to understand. Instead of God's great plans the
pious often see only their own little ideals. Over-
curious apologetics have been discredited and justly
so. But the great fundamental thought remains: God
reigns. It is retained by the faith of the heart, even
though our dim eyes cannot clearly see the application. Most clearly have all the devoted champions of
history and the historians of genuine genius appre-
hended it. One of their rare but weighty confessions
may here be heard: "Do the laws of human progress
proceed on their undisturbed march through the
ages in accordance with, or contrary to, the will of
the acting personalities or nations? What are these
laws? No one knows their inner nature, but their
results can be traced more or less clearly, if one
listens attentively to the voice of the past. At times,
in the manner in which events establish their own
connection, we gain a glimpse of something which
resembles a human face, shining with a smile both

stern and mild over the nations, which although they think themselves marching in ways of their own choosing, always arrive at goals at which they did not aim. If this glimpse is an illusion, it has nevertheless awakened the surmise, that the implacable laws of evolution are in reality not a system of rules of mechanism, but expressions of a personal will, against which no other can prevail. And in the centre of the history of the world, there arises a personality, which is not like any that we know. He points forward to a goal, toward which all the devious ways of the peoples are drawn together in a peace, which exceeds all their plans and dreams. Faith in Christ is a power for progress and life, which since his day has ruled the world, even against its will, and which strengthens those wills which are devoted to his service."[1] Denmark received in Grundtvig a prophetic spirit, for whom history, the past, the present and the future was the workshop of God. He interpreted the signs of the times. He advised and judged his people according to the promptings of the Spirit. He showed his people their place in the merciful providence of God. Edward Leh-

---

[1] Harald Hjärne, *Gustaf Adolfs minne,* in "Svenskt och Främmande," p. 55 ff.

man has left to his own and coming generations his book about Grundtvig as an inheritance which puts them in his debt. It is perhaps his most beautiful work, certainly an utterance which sets Grundtvig in the line of the prophets of all times, not merely the four major and the twelve minor prophets in Israel, but "monks and nuns from the cloisters of the North and the South, Russian peasants, English labourers, American folk preachers, highly cultivated writers, a Francis of Assisi, a St. Birgitta, a George Fox, a Joseph Smith, a Thomas Carlyle, a Dostoievski, prophets for today and for tomorrow, as for past millenniums." To show what a prophetic eye Grundtvig had for history we note the remarkable fact, that the last thing which the aged man requested be read to him on the day of his death, the Fourteenth Sunday after Trinity, September 1, 1872, after he had returned home from the church in Vartorv where he had preached, was Geijer's *The History of the Swedish People,* and *Historical Archives.* Lehman recognizes in him the true prophetic inspiration, intuition and vision. Moreover, the vocation of judge also was given to Grundtvig. He arose, as did the prophets of Israel, and preached repentance and spoke the truth with courage. He pronounced severe judgements, as did Jeremiah, even against his own wishes, and contrary to the kindness of his heart. Love was the deep, the divine element in his nature. And yet, in spite of all, he looked into the future with unconquerable hope, through his power of inspiration and his Christian faith. He cast his eye back to the beginning of time. He looked forward to its consummation. He learned to see God's will in the saga of Denmark as well as in the history of the world as a whole. The kingdom is coming, the millennium. This seer of the Northland was a true interpreter of the apocalyptic scenes of the book of Revelation (1930).

Heaven is not closed since the days of the Bible. The Christian sees heaven open in the Bible as nowhere else, and when darkness threatens to engulf him, he turns to its pages to find the eternal light penetrating the dark shadows. God's revelation, however, continues throughout all time. Thus far we agree with Roman Catholic doctrine. At this point, however, an important difference arises. Romanism says: "God continues his revelation in an institution which culminates in the Pope." We say: "God's continuing revelation is in men, in history." We too believe that the Church is the creation and instrument of God. The religious significance of the Church can be overrated, it is true, but it can also be under-rated. God has committed to the Church the divine privilege and the awful responsibility of communicating the grace of God to the world in word and deed and sacrament. Our belief in a continued revelation in history compels us to acknowledge, with greater conscientiousness and reverence than ever, the value of persons and of means and of institutions with which the divine guidance has provided our churches in the ordinances of history. But the Church ought to be more open-eyed than it is to the vision of God's continued revelation of himself. The Protestant doctrine that God has revealed himself pre-eminently in the Bible, and perhaps also through the sacraments, is true, and must be realized with renewed power. At the same time, it must not be forgotten that the chief lesson of the Bible itself is that God is a living God and has not grown aged or less active now than in his younger days. The Roman view finds the Biblicism of the Protestant narrow-minded, and says: "God is in his Church, he speaks through the ecclesiastical authority." At the same time that authority severs all connection with real history and buries itself in desperation in a mausoleum of antiquated thoughts and obsolete ideas. Against the Roman doctrine we raise two objections: 1) It makes the continued revelation of God leave the ground of history and become institutionalized; 2) It permits the continued revelation of God to abandon the area of life and shuts it up in a theological system, which was once alive, but is now only a venerable memorial of the past. God reveals himself in history outside the Church as well as inside of it. Was not Cyrus, the Pagan ruler, called Messiah by the prophet? God reveals himself in the destiny of peoples as well as in the institutions of religion. Standing on the Acropolis with the eye gliding over the Gulf of Saronica, along the bold lines of the coast from Cape Sunium in the bend of Eleusis back of Salamis, one may ask oneself which had the greater significance for the history of the reign of God on the earth, Marathon and Salamis, where the Athenians fought for their state, or Eleusis, farthest back in the stillness of the bay, where they sought comfort against mortality? It may come to pass, one can never know, that in some situations statesmen may be of greater significance for the kingdom of God than many thousands of preachers. It is possible for a few dreaming and acting Utopians to accomplish more for the purposes of God than the most glorious hierarchy or the best balanced and reputable piety, which calls those others mad. It may happen that political changes now in the Far East, the union of spiritual and material forces in a more comprehensive mutual influence and competition, the leveling of culture, such as is shown in the fact that the same curriculum is followed in the university of Shansi as in the university of Paris, the sharper competition between the great types of life going on under the surface, or again the influx of social movements in our own civilization, constitute a mightier revelation of God than any undertaking of the churches. God is able to speak to humanity even through lips which deny his existence. These sentences of mine are not intended as paradoxes, they are meant to be taken in actual literalness. In the complex progress of events only he can see the will of God, who takes his part in the struggle, and feels responsibility for the values involved. Suddenly the fog may lift. He is able to make out what is taking place. There are movements of the times in which it is difficult for any Christian with an open eye not to see the work of God. Through these world movements Christianity is brought both theoretically and practically to a test. Is it alive, does it think, does it act in the presence of the living God? Or is it shut up within the cheap self-satisfactions of little cliques, in a sort of esoteric artificiality or a dead scholastic interest? Does it possess receptivity for divine influences or has it settled upon the lees of its forms, habits, impulses?

The consciousness of a divine working in history has not arisen from the contemplation of the course of events and the motive powers of civilization, but out of a central religious experience of a personal character in the prophets. Belief in a revelation lives at all times under the same conditions. Geijer found it terrible "that the conception of order will be lost, if it is found possible to prove it only from material existence." It is easy to show that the fundamental idea in our civilization, namely *evolution,* comes out of the Biblical revelation on which our civilization thus lives, however far removed the optimism of our modern enthusiasts for evolution may be from the judgment proclamations of the prophets. It is clearly evident that philosophic thought concerning the events and progress of the world, if it proceeds from materialistic premises, invariably lands us in the doctrine of eternal cycles. This is true of our own philosophy as well as of that of other cultures.

The amiable heroes of civilization, or, shall we say slaves of civilization who believe that they can reject the fundamental Biblical idea of revelation and yet rejoice in progress, are guilty of a happy inconsistency. There are those also who deny, theoretically, the authority of the prophets, and yet are true successors of the prophets, for they sincerely and unselfishly exert their powers for the betterment of the world in the future. A sufficiently far-sighted and thorough-going analysis of culture can with difficulty escape the insight, that the only thing which gives, or can give, a soul to the restless body of Western education and technique and save our civilization, with its strivings, from self-contradiction and self-destruction, is the certainty that existence in its reality is Will, creative Will, with a revelation and a way of life founded upon that certainty. However, just as such an insight, in its historical beginning in the prophets of Israel and in Zoroaster—we have no proofs of any earlier origin—did not arise out of speculation about human culture and history, but out of the personal mysticism of communion with God, so at all times its origin must be in personalities who have religiously and historically lived themselves into and retained in an effective way this certainty. It does not have its foundation in conclusions drawn from the outward course of events and from the conditions of culture, but rather in the conflicts and victories of the inner personal life. Humanity must through anguish of soul and by the attraction of spiritual power, be forced *out* of history and civilization, and must feel the power of God in order to learn to see the revelation of God *in* history.

III

From the men of creative genius and from history we now pass to the third area of the continued revelation of God, the re-creation of the individual human being. What is the essential significance of the fact that a person becomes a Christian? We answer, two things. First, that a creation takes place within him, something original manifests itself in him in a measure analogous to the emergence of genius. Second, that he consciously enters into the historical progress of revelation.

1. God creates something new in the individual life. We have caught a glimpse of that mysterious continuation of the process of creation which reveals

itself in men of unique endowment. But in men and women of only ordinary powers something can happen which is akin to the phenomenon of genius. The resemblance does not consist in any peculiar intuitive or ecstatic working of the mind. In any case this is not the essential likeness. On the whole we must guard against giving peculiar and unusual psychical manifestations a value which they only apparently possess. The resemblance consists in the results achieved, that something relatively new and original emerges. This consists in a new freedom which is won through the complete subordination under the will of God. Ethical independence, the spiritual individuality, the "new man," is no more made according to prescription than the work of genius is produced according to a ready-made rule. In the "new man" there appears a life that is raised above Nature and possesses its principle within itself. When a man, heart-broken and repentant, turns resolutely from sin; when a soul in sincerity throws itself on the condemning and redeeming mercy of God; when a person, in spite of compulsion, temptation or calculation simply does his duty; when he concentrates himself in whole-hearted prayer; when in temptation and confusion clarity wins the victory;

when personality vindicates its freedom, then, in that sacred hour, there is produced a new creation. In conversion, in the birth to a new life, when truth, with sincerity and without sentimental softness is reckoned with in the inner life, the soul is lifted by the power of God to the heights of moral life and of communion with God, to a life which in its newness is akin to genius. I quote with pleasure the words of Kierkegaard, that "life is a poem which we ourselves are to write, but the Christian allows God to write his life's poem for him."

How essential moral independence is for Christianity is evident, among other facts, in its acknowledged relation to the most intimate and unfailing religious mark of Christian piety, namely the prayer of the heart. The specific proof of genuine answer to prayer, real prayer, not simply suggestion by means of psychological or mechanical methods, has traditionally been found in the fact that God has been revealed, not only in a certain emotional mood, but in a new power to overcome sin and difficulty. The great men of prayer in Christendom have not been content to make a sense of increased vital power in favourable conditions the ethical criterion of answer to prayer, nor rest from weariness, nor powers of concentration in the midst of division and confusion. They have found it rather in the fact that prayer has brought them strength in the struggle against satanic temptations, peace of mind enabling them to work in the midst of storming attack, bitter misunderstanding and terrible misfortunes; in the experience of quiet trust when spirit and body have been vexed, and in great spiritual rewards through suffering. No truth has found a clearer expression in modern times than the truth that moral independence belongs to the essence of Christianity. Kant is in this matter the authoritative interpreter of the Gospel. It is incontrovertible that, whether we condemn or approve, we find in the Kantian doctrine of the majesty and absoluteness of the ethical demand the product, or rather the fulfilment, of the metaphysical ground of the Christian ethic. Kant's poverty-stricken "Religion within the limits of mere Reason" is at one point profound and wonderful. In the presence of the fundamental fact of the moral life Kant bows in the dust and worships. There, without hesitation, he yields absolute reverence and obedience. Wilhelm Herrmann has moved away from Kant and yet maintained the same direction. He has

taken the final step. He has not paused in the purely
formal absoluteness of the demand of conscience. He
leads the soul on to Christ, in whom the demand receives a concrete content, which judges and puts man
to death just so long as he thinks himself able to care
for himself in his own strength, but which brings
about a divine creation in him, namely trust in the
mercy of God, so soon as he permits God to take
him by the hand.

When we thus, from certain points of view, draw a
parallel between the ethical liberation of the individual and the phenomenon of creative genius,[1] this does
not mean that we fail to appreciate the fact that the
moral life holds a unique place as compared with
that which is merely natural or produced by culture
only, or as compared with certain other elements in
human life which are expressions only of a highly
gifted personality. Actually there is an essential difference between a personal life animated from within by a spiritual and moral renewal, and a human
existence which lacks such a point of departure exalted above mere nature. This difference may be

---

[1] A masterly description of the power of spiritual awakening to lift
a human being out of ordinary powers into a higher existence is given
from actual life in Selma Lagerlöf's, *A Fallen King*.

established by observing the hierarchies of life accessible to us. Nevertheless, the moral life, when we find it exalted above mere legality or customary morality into personal independence, reveals striking analogies to the creation of genius. In the case of both, in the moral character as well as in genius, there is at hand a norm, not in the shape of outward rule, but as an inward principle, the working of which cannot be determined beforehand, but which, in its every function, constitutes its own rule, and when it comes to expression reveals a cohesion and a beauty in accordance with its peculiar variety of life. To consider the norm as being merely a pattern in accordance with which something is formed, is to misinterpret the creative power of genius and the essential being of the personal life as well. This inner principle, of the work of art or of the ethical personality, manifests itself in both as absolute, as a compulsion which is not like that of instinct or of some outward restraint that enslaves, degrades and finally destroys that unity of personality which is a mark of the mature ethical person. It is rather an absolute compulsion which, when obeyed, either in the fire of genius as it creates or in the labours and decisions of the life of conscience, conquers, exalts and confirms freedom and inner unity. This absolute compulsion of an inner principle reveals a third point of similarity. In both there is the common mark of life that it is a continuing creation which constantly brings forth that which is new. Even in the primitive stages of religion the initiation into the mysteries of the tribe means that the young initiate is held to have died and been born again into a new and higher life, so that he is in reality "twice-born." The endlessly varying symbolism of death and resurrection to a higher life found in the terminology of the mystery cults and religion, receives a new and more definite and noteworthy meaning when it is applied to moral renewal. "The new man" is more than a mere figure of speech. It is a revelation of the upward striving of the process of creation.

2. The Christianity of the individual signifies further, that revelation continues its history in him. He finds that his life means a choice between alternatives,—shall the creative power of God or shall the destructive power of evil rule his inner life? The movement of the great world drama seizes upon the individual soul. No neutrality is possible in the tremendous contradiction between life and death, crea-

tion or ruin. Every human soul must take its part in the struggle. At the same time the individual is made a part of that history of revelation which has already transpired. The history of God's dealings in the past becomes a history of God's present dealing with that particular soul. This history of the past becomes his own present history. "It happened for me." "Given and shed for you"—the most important event in the life of the individual is Jesus Christ. Not only so. Everything which takes place in the little history of the individual soul finds a new meaning, it becomes the dealing of God with his child.

Herein lies the Christian conception of *miracle*. An event in the outer or it may be in the inner life takes place. Or some person is found to constitute in a measure a divine revelation, and as such is seen to belong to a higher world than that of cause and effect as established by science. For the so-called primitive view, as well as for paganism and for remainders of ancient thought still surviving in our Christian civilization, miracle is that which we cannot understand. For Christian faith miracle is the opposite, it is, namely, that which faith really understands. We must examine this essential difference a little more closely. A man dies. No arrow struck him, no lion killed him, no waters drowned him. For the primitive man the case is one of mystery, magic, witchcraft; a powerful, mysterious and dangerous force or will must have been involved in the matter. On a higher plane of culture events and phenomena are connected together in a comprehensive system, but essentially the same attitude of mind may continue. An amazing happening, an unusual case, a fact that cannot be explained, is ascribed to a direct action by a spirit or god or to the supernatural powers of some man, and thus becomes a miracle. The mind of antiquity held a miracle to be a wonder—that which was unexplained or could not be explained. "Miracle is that which awakens amazement, whether it rises above nature or not." (Forcellini.) The miraculous was the same as the strange, a prodigy, an omen, a fearful mystery, that which by its magnitude or its beauty awakens amazement. Church writers gave the word a special meaning by reason of the dominating conception of God. Miracle was for them that which exceeded the powers of created nature, or that which happened contrary to the usual order and which is originated by God alone. This ecclesiastical conception held that the essential thing in a miracle was that it was inexplicable in the order of nature. This natural-historical point of view dominated in spite of the Christian idea of God, or at least it was of equal force with the religious idea. This is evident, characteristically, in the definitions of St. Thomas Aquinas, which, essentially, have been retained by evangelical scholasticism. In his *Summa Theologiae* [1] he defines the concept miracle, as "that which happens outside of the order of nature known to us, in which sense God alone can work miracles." If the wonderful event does not fall outside of the area of nature, although it exceed our knowledge, it is a miracle only for us, but not in itself (*quoad nos, sed non simpliciter*). In his apologetic work, *Summa contra Gentiles or Summa philosophica,*[2] St. Thomas differentiates in the same way between that which is simply marvellous, *simpliciter mirum,* the cause of which may be hidden from one person and known to another, and the miracle, the cause of which is known to no human being in this life, for it is of God and not of Nature. "By miracle then is meant

---

that which is wrought by God, outside the general order of things." [1] The dominating point of view in this definition also is the negative one, namely that man cannot grasp the cause, for it is God and not Nature. This dualism of God and Nature, of the Creator and his creation, is still more marked in the three grades of miracles indicated by St. Thomas. The highest grade is that miracle in which God does something which Nature never can do, as when two bodies occupy the same space, or the sun goes backward or stands still, or a path appears in the sea by which we may cross it. The next grade is that miracle in which God works that which Nature also can do, but not in the same order, as when a creature lives after death, receives his sight after blindness, etc. The third and lowest grade is that miracle in which God does that which Nature is wont to do, but without using the powers of Nature, as when one is healed of a curable sickness by divine power, or when it rains without the ordinary working of Nature. The miracle therefore consists in the fact that God acts, setting aside the causal order which he has instituted and which constitutes the created

---

[1] "Illa igitur simpliciter miracula dicenda sunt quae divinitus fiunt praeter ordinem communiter servatum in rebus."

order of Nature. God is present in the causal order as its ultimate cause, whereas in the miracle he suspends those causes which are near at hand and accessible to our knowledge, and intervenes directly, without their mediation. Augustine produced another doctrine of miracle out of his Platonic premises. For him everything was practically equally miraculous, for the all-penetrating creative power of God is everywhere present. For man, however, certain unusual events, proceeding from the eternal resources of God, are miracles. They cannot, indeed, be contradictory of Nature, for Nature is the work of God himself. The contradiction lies in our own understanding, which is limited to the usual processes of Nature. The conception of miracle held by St. Thomas, under the influence of the Aristotelian world view, with its antithesis between the created causal order and the intervention of God as prompted by his government of the universe, gained precedence as the orthodox view of the Church and found its final expression in the conception of miracle as the temporary suspension of Nature's laws. This conception of miracle makes of it something which is fundamentally indifferent ethically and religiously. This is not so clearly seen in the stricter conception of miracles held by the Scholastics, in which miracle lies outside of the possibilities of Nature and is reserved for God alone. It is more clearly evident in their wider conception of miracle, according to which even the devil works wonders. Of course the religious point of view is not altogether lacking, as when Augustine differentiates between that which merely arouses surprise (*ludicra*) and that which results in great good (*utilia*), or when the Scholastics differentiate between the amazing work of the devil and the miracles of God, the latter of which aim at the confirmation of the truth [1] and the salvation of men. The miracle belongs to the divine government of the world. Even in this conception, however, the religious significance is not permitted to break through the ancient natural view.

This had, however, been done long before in the Bible, already even in those books and sayings of the Old Testament, which are saturated with the spirit of Mosaism and prophetism, for which miracle has the meaning of acts of God for the purpose of salvation. It is true that the view of revealed religion is sometimes fused with the primitive, popular conception of miracles, yet it is dominating throughout,

---

[1] Ex. J. Gerhard, *Systema, De ecclesia*, sectio XI.

and not seldom it emerges in its purity. The place of honour is held by the marvellous works done in times of old, with similar ones in the history of the people both before and after the Exile, so long as the religious spirit possessed sufficient spiritual sensitiveness or there were personalities to interpret these events. But events in the individual or social life, also, yes, in all that God has done, in Nature as well as in the Law,[1] are miracles for him whose eyes have been opened to see the work of God. The fundamental idea of the Biblical religions is not cult or piety, but revelation. In the New Testament, the "mighty" works of Jesus are done in his vocation, in the service of love and the rule of God, in contrast to "signs and wonders." In that strictly supernatural view which marks Christianity, God's work and God's world as a whole are miracles, if in them there is revealed the gracious will of God. This will of God, not that of phenomenal causes, is the true world order. Thus miracle for revealed religion, is not that which cannot be understood, not that which merely arouses wonder, but rather that which only faith understands. In the measure that faith is conscious of the presence of God and sees a

---

[1] Ps. 19. Cf. E. Billing quoted above.

divine purpose in that which is happening, the event is unveiled as a miracle and viewed as a revelation.[1] E. G. Geijer wrote to Fredrika Bremer, November 9, 1842: "We say a miracle, not in the sense of the inexplicable, but in the sense of that which is explicable only through itself." "That it is not ignorance which makes the miracle is best shown in this, that investigation does not remove the miraculous in it, but rather brings it to the consciousness with the sense of reality."

Much, perhaps we may say most, of all that happens in Nature and human life is either without interest to us, or is obscure and puzzling, or even tempts us to doubt and mistrust. It is possible that there is really nothing mysterious in all these happenings. The causal connection is possibly as clear and natural and commonplace as can be. Or it may still be true that, for scientific explanation, real difficulties are to be found in these events. But for faith, however, they are dead, meaningless or puzzling, disturbing. Faith cannot find in them a spiritual connection. Faith does not understand in them a purpose of God. The event may be strange, it may

---

[1] Cf. N. J. Göransson, *Gudsförhållandets kristologiska grund,* II, Upsala 1910, p. 100 ff.

awaken questioning and prompt investigation, but it is no miracle in the religious sense. Where faith speaks of miracle, there faith is at home, there it understands and knows, that God has done this for the salvation of man, to give aid and comfort to those who are concerned. The event in question may constitute an everlasting problem for science, as does, for example, the person of Jesus, or the origins of Christianity. Or again the event may be the most natural thing in the world, a happening in some individual life, unimportant for others, momentous for him who experiences it. From the religious point of view, the event is full of meaning and content, for here God meets man, God is making himself known to humanity or to the individual. This meeting with God belongs to the world of the inner life, yet it is bound up with history, finds its analogy chiefly with the appearing of Christ. Science must take note of it. It finds perhaps, that such a miracle or revelation-element, which has become so significant, yes, revolutionary, for the outward formation of life and history, belongs to a mighty kingdom of reality. It would be an insult to science as well as to religion, should we seek to apply the religious interpretation instead of the natural or scientific. Religion moves in a deeper region of reality. Its miracles do not mean simply a temporary break in the causal chain. The religious miracle is something positive, God's action, not something negative, the unintelligible.

For Christ all was miracle; that is, He saw the work of God everywhere. Nothing was for Him dead or meaningless. The heroes and saints of Christendom also have been able to see the hand of God and have fellowship with the Divine, where the ordinary man, thoughtless and blind, has walked unseeing through the very miracles of God all about him.

———

The difference between the general science of religion and Christian theology is this, that for the latter, faith in revelation is essential. For Christian theology, the history of religion is at the same time a divine self-disclosure. The general science of religion leaves the question of revelation open. A scholar may be animated by the conviction that behind the phenomena of religion lies a supramundane reality; or, he may deny that which is fundamental for religion, namely faith in a spiritual reality; or, he may stand questioning and uncertain about revelation, perhaps certain only of the impos-

sibility of knowing anything about it; or, he may
lack interest entirely in the question of the truth of
religion. Naturally different attitudes toward the idea
of revelation must not be allowed to influence the
method of scientific investigation in historical and
psychological enquiries, so that these come to be distorted by dogmatism one way or the other. The cure
for such mistakes cannot lie in the prohibition of any
conviction on the part of the investigator. It lies
simply in the correct aim of the investigation, conscientious precision and seriousness in the process,
and in the readiness of the scientific spirit to bow
before the actual fact.

In the Biblical faith in revelation, there is indeed
included the conviction that one part of the history
of religion constitutes revelation in a more real and
a richer sense than in the history of religions in general. This doctrine of a special revelation must, however, be tested in the light of historical reality. So
much can be established by a sufficiently thorough
orientation, that the claim of a special revelation
within the general revelation, which is made by the
Biblical faith, answers to that special type of religion,
which we have called, in the terminology of Usener,
revealed religion. With this term we have not meant

to express any view of the metaphysical problem concerning divine self-disclosure. We simply verify the
historical and psychological peculiarity of the prophetic, or personal, or vocational religions. This type
of religion, revealed religion, is traced back to the
special psychological conditions mentioned in the
second chapter, and possesses the peculiar quality set
forth in the first chapter.[1] The characteristic and essential difference between this religion and the con-

---

[1] Henri Bergson had accepted two years before the World War an in-
vitation by the Olaus Petri Foundation to deliver a series of lectures at
the University of Upsala. This brought about a correspondence concerning the theme of these lectures, which were to treat of the application of his fundamental philosophical tenets as to history and man,
more especially his theory of "creative evolution." I asked him if he
knew of any connection between this and the prophetic conception of
history. For everywhere except in the religion of the prophets or in revealed religion, history becomes fundamentally meaningless, a repetition
of the same things, sin and misery, and a saviour for different epochs,
which, in what one might call an astronomic vastness, follow one upon
another in the ancient cosmology of the Hindus, with parallels in the
thought of Greece and of China. A goal for history and for progress of
the world is found only in the prophetism of the Old and New Testament from which the creations of Islam and Zoroaster have inherited
the conception of purpose in the world. Bergson answered that he did
not know of this connection but the thought appealed to him and he
would make a closer examination of it. When the eminent disciple of
Bergson, Professor Jacques Chevalier visited Upsala last year, the
conversation centred on the postulates of Bergson's philosophy. I mentioned to him my surmise. I received the answer that a prominent
French critic had discovered that Bergson was Jewish in his doctrine.
The critic's opinion testifies to a correct orientation. For the conception
that Reality, Being, is symbolized by such terms as purpose, will, creation, realization, penetration, progress, power, energy, life, has its source
in the religion of the prophets (1930).

ceptions of the ancient world in general may be clearly recognized by a cultural-historical analysis today, in such modern lines of thought as are consciously or unconsciously continuations of revealed religion.[1]

But if the Christian faith has thus marked off a certain area as belonging to special revelation, and this, to a certain extent, is analogous to that which the science of religion does when it marks off revealed religion as a unique type within the history of religion, this does not mean that the distinction is an absolute one in time and space. Neither does the science of religion do away with the fact of the affinity of all religions, when it separates them for scientific study. Actually this connection of all forms of religion into unitary groups of phenomena, answers to the prophetic and Christian faith in a divine self-disclosure to the nations outside "the chosen people" or the influence of Christianity. In other writings I have sought to show that there is a Christian faith in a divine influence even outside the area of special revelation, in different nations and cul-

---

[1] Cf. *Religionsproblemet,* by Söderblom, II, p. 235 ff., 415 ff., and for the question of the Portals of Religion cf. *Religionsproblemet,* II. p. 258 ff.

tures. Wherein the element of revelation in any particular form of religion consists, is difficult to say; it becomes impossible if one attempts to apply an intellectualistic view. But the *fact* that there is a measure of revelation, that is, of a divine self-disclosure, wherever there is found a sincere religiousness, is expressed by faith in a revelation, which is held both within and without the Christian religion.[1]

In the foregoing pages the attempt has been made to indicate the universal application of faith in revelation, as regards time. As surely as the Christian faith holds that the divine self-impartation lies open before us, valid and inexhaustible for all time, in the sacred history and above all in the personality of Christ, equally impossible is it to hold fast to faith in revelation without extending it beyond the times of the Bible. Naturally it has been possible only to sketch the outlines here. To attempt a detailed map of the continued revelation is difficult. One incurs danger of profanation or of subjectivism. It is desirable and necessary, however, that this conviction of a continuing revelation be filled with a concrete content and that we try to interpret its meaning.

The three essential elements which have been pre-

---

[1] *Religionsproblemet* by Söderblom, II, p. 445 ff., 454 ff.

sented, namely genius, history, and the spiritual personality, constitute in my opinion the most important points of view for classification in the history of religion as a whole. The phenomenon of monotheism is not such a point of view. This may more often be a striving after unity in the theoretical study of religions, or of political life, rather than of religious movement. Nor is the general progress of morals more promising. This progress certainly does proceed with reciprocal influence from and upon religion, but it is by no means identified with the development of religion. These elements are concerned with 1) the fact that religion, on various stages and in various senses, is bound up with a hero, a saviour and a prophet, more especially a divine personality working in the world, whether it be a deified man or a humanized, mythical creation, or a Christ; 2) the relation of religion to history; and 3) the place of the ethical values within the conception of salvation and all acts of worship and work, of life itself.